Strategic alternatives to exclusion from school

REVISED AND UPDATED EDITION

Strategic alternatives to exclusion from school

REVISED AND UPDATED EDITION

Carl Parsons

Trentham Books

Stoke on Trent, UK and Sterling, USA

Trentham Books Limited
Westview House   22883 Quicksilver Drive
734 London Road   Sterling
Oakhill   VA 20166-2012
Stoke on Trent   USA
Staffordshire
England ST4 5NP

First published 2009
Revised edition 2011

British Library Cataloguing-in-Publication Data
A catalogue record for this book is available from the British Library

ISBN: 978 1 85856 499 9

Designed and typeset by Trentham Books Ltd
Printed and bound in Great Britain by 4edge Limited, Hockley

Contents

Instruments available on the web at
http://www.gre.ac.uk/__data/assets/pdf_file/0016/
511630/resrcs-alternative-tools.pdf

1 Local authority needs assessment and audit of assets tool
2 Headteacher interview schedule
3 Parent interview schedule
4 Pupil interview schedule

Acknowledgements

My thanks go first to the Esmée Fairbairn Foundation for the bulk of the financial support and particularly Hilary Hodgson who advised on how the project should be shaped, the financial partnership which should be sought with local authorities (LAs) and the goals it should state explicitly.

I owe a great deal to the changing team (listed below) which worked with me over the course of the project and to Deborah Ghate, director of the Policy Research Bureau, which was where the project was conceived and was based for its early stage before moving with me to Canterbury Christ Church University. Subsequent work has been managed from my location in the Research Centre for Children, Schools and Families at the University of Greenwich.

I would like to thank the personnel from the eight LAs who participated in the development project and particularly the five 'high excluding' LAs which were the focus of our work and which contributed financially. The LAs involved gave considerable attention to the goals of the exercise and sought to guide us to people and institutions in their area where a difference to exclusion rates might be made. It has to be acknowledged that developments are swift and the LAs have all moved forward in different ways, partly because of changed national conditions and the reformulation of services for children and families and partly through local, targeted efforts to reduce exclusions. We hope the outcomes will be of interest and significance to the all LAs and others around the country which are working towards inclusion.

The report represents a developing picture across the LAs. I hope that, in the changing environments that we are all experiencing, the text does justice to the accounts people gave and the analysis presented.

If there is a dedication, it is to a better and fairer system for education and care of children instead of exclusion and punishment. The project team learnt the chastening lesson that itinerant, external 'experts' can do little and that solutions lie within LAs, with committed elected members, determined and energetic officers, headteachers, teachers and statutory services working together robustly and with good will. As change agents, they can, however, give impetus, legitimation and some new ideas on structures, roles, emphases and pace that support the local efforts to reduce exclusions.

I must finally thank the staff of Trentham books for agreeing to this second edition which allows for an update on progress towards zero permanent exclusions. It also enables adjustments to the text to take account of the new conditions which prevail under the coalition government which came into office in May 2010.

Project Team

Carl Parsons (Director); Hanan Hauari; Adam Abdelnoor (from 01.04.08); Yang Tian (until 30.03.07); Helen Monteiro (until 30.03.07); Keith Howlett (from 01.04.08)

'Exclusion from school, either permanently or for a fixed period, is a quiet mockery of *Every Child Matters*.' (this book, p7)

Foreword

Adam Abdelnoor

Carl Parsons is absolutely right to condemn exclusion as a 'quiet mockery of *Every Child Matters*'. We need fully to appreciate the devastating effect of permanent exclusion on children and families. Though schools are not doing it consciously, the excludee is the scapegoat for our failure to make sure every child matters. Do we mean every child matters? For instance, though government guidelines already say schools must do all they can to avoid exclusion, many schools have excluded children permanently whilst sitting on substantial cash reserves. Can they really claim to have 'done everything possible' before excluding when those reserves could have funded an alternative programme for the child, off-site if necessary? So *do* we mean every child matters, or do we not?

Most of us have heard, on many occasions, something said to this effect: 'I failed my eleven-plus and it spoiled my life chances'. Twenty or more years on, this 'failure' still hurts them. Those of us who work with excluded communities hear a similar story from parents of excluded children who were themselves excluded. The hurt, the negative impact on opportunities, expectations and achievement, and the stigma are long lasting and perhaps, as the name implies, permanent. Worse, they seem to have a detrimental effect for the next generation, too.

Just as public opinion in favour of hanging is unlikely to change state opposition to it, so public opinion about 'being tough on feral youths' and similar attitudes should not influence the response of those directing, managing and delivering services to children. Children may be on the margins and at risk of exclusion for many reasons. Mostly, they have developmental problems, and it is now widely recognised that these are frequently linked to difficulties with attachment – the ability to trust, to belong, and to sustain positive relationships. From a mental health perspective, mainstream expert opinion is clear:

coercive strategies are contraindicated for children with attachment problems. Punishment – for that is what exclusion is – is not appropriate.

Such children need help to develop into adults who have a good chance of good health, success, and the opportunity to make a positive contribution to society. Intervention becomes much harder after adolescence. They and their families need more support, not less, not only for their sake but also for the wider community's sake. None of us want disturbed and confused children acting out in our society or the heavy costs associated with it. For all these reasons, the energetic pursuit of better alternatives to exclusion is necessary, valuable and right.

The research shows that from time to time exclusion rates in a particular school drop dramatically. For instance, in one school permanent exclusions fell from eleven to zero in the space of a year. This is very unlikely to be because the pupils' behaviour had suddenly changed for the better, and indeed behind this true story is the story of a Damascus moment: the headteacher suddenly saw a better way, and followed it. Similar dramatic changes in exclusion rates year on year can be seen in at LA level, too.

There do seem to be at least two key dynamics at work *other than the pupils' behaviour.* These sudden significant reductions in exclusions followed organisational changes at school and local authority level, and attitudinal changes in the key people involved.

This book is about both of these things, but focuses especially on the organisational and attitudinal changes required at the *community level.* This obviously means the Local Authority, which is deeply involved in the process. However, in community terms the LA is a strategic partner rather than its control centre. This community is 'everyone involved in providing children's services'. Nor should we confuse 'community' with 'association' – mere proximity does not create community. Communality of need creates community. When what happens to you directly effects what happens to me, I am bound to be more concerned about your well-being. This mutuality of need is the driver for greater co-operation, joined up thinking, and more importantly, joined up people'.

Addressing the needs of marginalised children without using exclusion will require co-operation between all the schools and agencies in the community to achieve a simple goal – that the needs of all the children in the community are met. After all, if not *within* the community, then where?

Would you want your neighbouring community's reject pupils?

There needs to be enough autonomy at the local learning network level to meet the alternative needs of all the community's children through what can be made available – schools, on-site and off-site units and other agencies and services. This can only be achieved by senior managers working together across organisational boundaries towards a common vision of diversity of provision, managed moves and an obvious goal – finding the *right* school places for *every* child. This vision of community engagement has its own simple mnemonic – broaden the schools, build the bridges and find a place for every child.

Within this mnemonic another principle is implicit – '*voluntariness*' is a powerful positive dynamic. Different organisations (such as schools, PRUs and psychology services) cannot be *made* to work effectively together because they have different organisational hierarchies and cultures. Inclusive education is the mark of a society that can afford to care and *chooses to do so.* Change is a process which starts when people become aware that *something needs changing.* Without this, there is a danger that the physical wall comes down only to be replaced with social barriers – a virtual social wall. Resistance to centralised planning can make changes ineffective, inefficient or unworkable. When managers across organisations and at all levels share a real vision with common goals ('the big picture') they can take responsibility for their part in making the vision a reality, and are more willing to go the second mile to make it happen. This requires courage in leadership, and a quantum shift in outlook from many of us who tend to focus on getting the detail right, action planning and project management – though these will need to happen too.

Courage is easier for leaders who have a good understanding of the management of transformative change, the kind of change that impacts on every aspect of community life including culture, politics, ethics and attitudes.

This inclusive community needs to be a *distributed community*, with different organisations working together to a common vision but not yoked together hierarchically. Whilst sceptics might doubt that a voluntary approach to building this community can be effective, voluntariness does confer enormous operational advantages if properly applied, and actually it doesn't work any other way, for the reasons given!

Avoiding exclusion is not a personal challenge to be met by individual teachers though we truly applaud those teachers willing to rise to it. It should not be about heroic headteachers standing fast against the pressures for exclusion – though we know of some headteachers who deserve that accolade. It's the collective responsibility of everyone at all levels including that of elected representatives to reconfigure and deliver educational provision within their local area which meets the needs of the full range of children eligible to receive that service.

This book is not about revoking the law that allows exclusion but about making exclusion unnecessary – obsolete, in fact. It's about our future society, about breaking the cycle of exclusion and the individual and financial cost it imposes on all of us. We can aim to reduce the numbers of adults who are disaffected, unhealthy, antisocial or incompetent – with consequent savings to the public purse and a healthier, safer, more prosperous, happier society. It is difficult to prove that programmes which focus on children's social and developmental problems achieve reductions in demand for services. Appropriate research protocols are difficult to devise and need to be very large if the statistics are to be reliable. In any case projections into the future can never provide the confidence which comes with having empirical data – we haven't got there yet! However, the reasoning sounds right and the cost benefits provide excellent leverage.

For instance, it would clearly provide substantial savings to support one young person now, who would otherwise have been excluded, so they can form prosocial relationships that change their personal and social competences, helping them stay out of prison or hospital, and to avoid the need for social care for them and their children. We need to find more ways to move the funding from *treatment* to *prevention*. That means not just early intervention but earlier intervention. Children who fail to thrive in school are giving us a very clear message. 'I need direct support *now*'. The more difficult the child the louder the shout – but the message is always the same.

Will it work? We should act with confidence. Where committed professionals are encouraged to engage creatively and positively with young people who need to have a period of intensive and individualised support before moving to an alternative programme or school, it does work. And politicians have their part to play in asserting and applying with firm conviction that children who are at risk from exclusion need help not punishment.

At the heart of effective inclusive practice we always found people with vision, commitment and determination. We found them in high excluding LAs and in low excluding ones. Whether they worked for the LA, school, PRU or other agency they shared a common attitude which can be best summed up in five words: ' Every child matters – to me'. It's the last two words which make a reality of the other three.

A deep well of compassion and concern for young people experiencing difficulties at school, frequently expressed in the form of challenging behaviour, has sustained the determination of the author of this book. He deserves to be congratulated and appreciated. In pooling the combined knowledge and understanding of committed professionals both from across the country and from across children's services, as well as parents and children themselves, his primary values have been diligence, objectivity and a global perspective. It has been extremely hard work, crossing the country time and time again to implement a field research programme over eighteen months covering eight widely dispersed LAs and analysing and interpreting a vast amount of data.

Interpreting this data-lake, and making sense of its complex arrays of statistics, individual views, documentation and field observation, has certainly been challenging. No doubt the views expressed here will be challenged. One observation may however be made with confidence – it is extremely unlikely that factors not covered in this book could explain why exclusions vary from school to school, LA to LA and region to region. If other factors were relevant, we would have been made aware of them by one of our hundreds of informants. The data is comprehensive as well as broad.

Adam Abdelnoor is founding chief executive of the inclusion charity Inaura and author of Managed Moves: A complete guide to managed moves as an alternative to permanent exclusion *(2008, Calouste Gulbenkian Foundation). www.inaura.net*

1

Introduction

Background

School exclusions have been for me a personal, professional and political concern for over 15 years. My opposition to school exclusion has been expressed as a school governor, as a friend and supporter for those who have experienced exclusion and their families, through publicity and lobbying and through research and writing on primary pupils excluded, monitoring rates of exclusion, costing exclusion, minority ethnic exclusion (Parsons *et al*, 2005; Parsons, 2008) and the national culture of exclusion (Parsons, 2004, 2010).

This project, *Strategic Alternatives to Exclusion from School*, set out to test and report on what works for LAs and schools in reducing exclusions and sustaining policies and practices to ensure the continued education of challenging children. The work was funded by the Esmée Fairbairn Foundation and by the five high excluding LAs. Their agreement to participate, sometimes expressed with enthusiasm, was itself a positive sign, indicating their recognition of the problem and corporate motivation to reduce it. The project lasted 18 months, from October 2006 to March 2008, and operated in three phases:

Phase 1 Examining national exclusions data and visits to three low excluding LAs

Phase 2 Needs assessment, auditing assets and working in five high excluding LAs

Phase 3 Consolidating, collective workshop and reporting

The Phase 1 activities allowed an exploration of available data on three low excluding local authorities (LAs) and the identification of key factors associ-

1

ated with low rates of exclusion in each area. It provided the opportunity to check hypotheses about the organisation and crucial elements of policy and practice which led to low official rates of permanent exclusions; it allowed an interrogation of up to date instances of broadened school provision, alternative curriculum and managed transfer. Attention was also given to Scotland which has consistently reported permanent exclusions at about 10 per cent of the rate experienced in England. Phase 1 confirmed the importance of the local authority dimension, political involvement and commitment and the need for a strong guiding and coordinating role for local authority personnel. In the three low excluding LAs, trust, speedy response and constructive, non punitive layers of provision were robustly coordinated, worked effectively and were impressive in their impact on exclusion statistics. Scotland also showed the power of national pressure and local cooperation.

Phase 2 focused on five high excluding English LAs. This involved important discussions with stakeholder groups to present a picture of where the problems of exclusions were most acute and what organisations played a part in addressing the needs of young people at risk of exclusion. The gathering of additional data following the first stakeholder meeting enabled the development of a fuller picture of provision, or lack of it, and how, across the five LAs, different factors played important parts: size of LA; small numbers of high excluding schools; the tension between speedy provision and rewarding threats of exclusion; inter-professional frictions; compromised political stances; finance.

The intention to engage in mini projects within each of the authorities was translated into further focused data gathering, rather than practical activities, with a small number of schools working to achieve new agreed measures to prevent exclusion. These further enquiries examined learning support units in one LA, primary exclusions in two LAs; the difficulties encountered in reducing exclusions in one district of one LA; and the possibilities of three secondary schools collaborating in the management of one PRU which they might use collectively to avoid recourse to exclusions.

The project aimed to reduce permanent and fixed term exclusions and to be an instrument for examining need and auditing assets in relation to school exclusions. Through the phase 3 workshop, it was possible to test out ideas about what worked. Of significance is the finding that, while the power of LAs may be diminished in the management of education, the determination to reduce exclusions is very much a local collective decision relying on cooperation between local authority officers, with political backing, and schools.

Consortia of schools, local learning partnerships or emerging local children's services partnerships were not visibly active forums for addressing matters of exclusion. A number of headteachers had shown how, with the right internal arrangements and external support, permanent exclusions could be minimised; they had changed from being relatively high excluders to being nil excluders. This generated optimism for effecting reductions in exclusion on a wide scale if the right local conditions can be created.

In fact there has been a fourth phase as the learning from the project has been disseminated, as new local authority and school cluster case studies have come in and with the new context of the coalition government's plans for the management of exclusions. This phase has involved articulating in more detail the essence of Community Based Inclusion.

The focus
The permanent and fixed term exclusion of young people from school, through a specific education law, is peculiarly British if not English. The removal of education, even for a short period, unless for the health and safety of the individual or the school community, would seem to be individually and socially damaging. Furthermore, exclusions are applied disproportionately to lower socio-economic groups and some ethnic groups, which raises social justice issues. Poorer children, as signified by free school meals entitlement, and those of Black Caribbean heritage are three times as likely to be excluded; this increased rate applies equally to permanent and to fixed term exclusions. The outcomes for permanently excluded young people are, in general, poor and it is vital to find other ways of managing the continued education and development of these young people.

This project focused on exclusions at LA level because analysis of education power and control suggests that there is a corporate level influence through elected members, personnel and the control of some resources. It was also as a result of two factors emerging from an analysis of national exclusions data: firstly, the top 15 LA excluders had an average exclusion rate of 0.21 per cent (2003/04 figures) while the 15 lowest excluders averaged 0.03 per cent permanent exclusions. The national average was 0.13 per cent. Secondly, low excluders appeared to be able to maintain their low excluder position over time and some high excluders had been in that category regularly over many years. There is, therefore, an LA dynamic at work. Though the LA is the central strategic partner it is best to think in terms of the education community dynamic which comprises a set of forces and agents which goes wider. If an LA's ways of working with its schools and other stakeholders can be strengthened and better targeted, it was reasoned that there should be a multiplier effect in reducing school exclusions.

The need to address exclusions locally and nationally

The number of permanent school exclusions in England has remained static at a little under 10,000 for the 10 years since 1999 (see Table 1.1 below). This national statistic hides a wide variation at LA level and further variations within local areas. According to DCSF figures for 2007/08 (always a year behind), the average rate of permanent exclusion across LAs was 0.11 per cent. DfE figures for 2008/09 showed a further, very substantial fall in numbers to 6,550, 0.09%. At the same time, the number of LAs recorded as zero or under 5 permanent excluders rose to 17 out of a total of 150 LAs.

Disruption and indiscipline in schools has to be addressed. But both the disproportionality of exclusions for some groups, notably the poor and those already marginalised, and the negative consequences lifelong for those who experience exclusion, plus the harm and cost falling on the wider society strongly suggest that better ways than excluding need to be found. Social cohesion is not helped by the present exclusionary and punitive approach.

The rate for fixed term exclusion rose from 344,500 reported incidents in 2003/04 to a peak of 425,600 in 2006/07, amounting to 5.7% of the school population – if pupils only received one fixed term exclusion each, which they

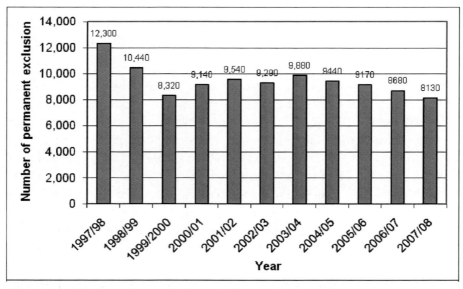

Figure 1.1: Permanent exclusions in England – 1997/8-2007/8

do not. Nonetheless, it is calculated that more than three pupils in a hundred experience a period of fixed term exclusion in the year. The numbers reduced to 363,000 in 2008/09. The total number of days lost to education is staggering.

A striking but overlooked phenomenon is the much lower rates of permanent exclusion which have persisted for years in the other constituent countries of the UK. Table 1.1 shows that in Wales permanent exclusion rates have been fairly low and often at half the rate for England. Scotland and Northern Ireland have done better, with rates which are a quarter of those in England. It is clear from both the figures and the commentaries on those countries' websites that a different commitment to the care and well-being of all children prevails.

	1997/98	1998/99	1999/2000	2000/01	2001/02	2002/03	2003/04	2004/05	2005/06	2006/07	2007/08	2008/09
N. Ireland	0.021	0.02	0.02	0.02	0.02	0.02	0.02	0.02	0.02	0.02	0.01	0.01
Scotland	0.018	0.02	0.06	0.05	0.05	0.05	0.03	0.05	0.04	0.04	0.02	0.02
Wales	0.103	0.06	0.05	0.06	0.06	0.06	0.06	0.07	0.06	0.05	0.07	0.04
England	0.172	0.14	0.11	0.12	0.13	0.12	0.13	0.13	0.12	0.12	0.11	0.09

Table 1.1: Percentage rates of permanent exclusion in the countries of the United Kingdom

There have been many adjustments to the DfEE/DfES/DCSF guidance on exclusions, first given in 1999, which attempted to balance support for school discipline with meeting the needs of often troubled and troublesome young people. Inevitably, the forces to drive down exclusions and protect all young people's rights to appropriate education are in tension with the punitive disciplinary messages. Neither government exhortation on the one hand nor highly skilled work on the ground with individuals and families will adequately address the exclusion issue. There needs to be work on the level of intermediate institutional power bases such as LAs and local school partnership groups.

Subsequently, the DfES made clear the challenges schools and LAs must meet. The Practitioners' Group report (Steer, 2005) on school behaviour and discipline recommended collaborations and local partnerships to manage the challenging behaviour of the few. The Department for Children, Schools and Families *Children's Plan* (DCSF, 2007a) expects headteachers collectively to develop on- and off-site alternative provision for suspensions longer than five days. The Secretary of State had earlier expressed the wish that 'Education Improvement Partnerships' (Teachernet, 2005) would operate to address disaffection, truancy and poor behaviour. The government's education website positively seethes with guidance (DfES, 2004a; 2004b; 2004c), revised guidance (DCSF, 2007a), holistic planning for children's brighter futures (DCSF, 2007b) and modernising educational provision (DCSF, 2008a). The Children's Plan 'expects secondary schools to be in behaviour partnerships' and they will be 'piloting new forms of alternative provision ...' (p84). The LA remains a significant player in four respects: firstly, the LA has retained funds which it uses for behaviour support, Pupil Referral Units (PRUs) and other centralised services; secondly, the LA has the legal responsibility to provide full-time equivalent education for pupils out of school from day 6 though some LAs and schools are not meeting this target for 100 per cent of permanent exclusions or longer fixed term exclusions (Ofsted, 2009); thirdly, the LA is the co-ordinating agent across the Children, Family and Education Service and has the job of commissioning from other agencies; fourthly, elected councillors have a powerful part in decisions locally about inclusion, support for young people and families and other matters of community ethos.

Much guidance is available on design principles and protocols on, for instance, hard to place children, fair access and managed moves (DCSF, 2007c). The Steer Report (2009) is a distillation of principles and actions for tackling bad behaviour in schools. It reminds schools of their legal powers and the importance of plain good teaching. It highlights the role of early intervention and links with parents but only comes close to going beyond the individual school when it discusses of the role of the behaviour and attendance partnerships and mentions the Children's Trusts and even CAMHS (child and adolescent mental health services). The emphasis is nonetheless on eradicating, or at least reducing, 'poor behaviour [which] cannot be tolerated as it is a denial of the right of pupils to learn and teachers to teach' (p3). The change is to be made to the pupil rather than the set of learning institutions. A strategic view of exclusions would embrace the whole local education community and be organising layers of provision to cater for all children rather than just making the pupils fit.

It could be the case that outside agents can only act as catalysts and supporters for what is very much an LA and school-based process of reducing exclusions. The external change agent role has a degree of objectivity. There is undoubtedly a collective dynamic at work, even if there is no apparent consensus, to judge from the diversity of an LA's school exclusion figures. How to intervene in the local dynamic most effectively is still the challenge. Government circulars and advisory material may be copious but exclusion rates have never been a major consideration in Ofsted inspections of LAs and they are still missing now in Joint Area Reviews (JARs). Local determination to be a low excluder, or a nil excluder, is nonetheless in evidence and part of the purpose of this study is to offer ways in which this might be spread. The position at the outset, and retained through the work, was not that schools should not be allowed to exclude but rather that exclusion should become unnecessary.

The English way seems to be pursued in ignorance of, or with a disinclination to look at, the situation in other countries. Even the other countries of the United Kingdom do not have exclusion rates on the English scale and the countries of mainland Europe do not have an educational law that permits a headteacher to exclude a child permanently from their school. It is a regarded as a matter of state decision-making, often resisting removal of a child from a school because of the state remit for schools to prepare all children for their roles as citizens, hopefully in good relationships and contributing productively as workers. Exclusion from school, either permanently or for a fixed period, is a quiet mockery of *Every Child Matters*. Exclusions have an interesting way of fuelling tensions between education and children's social services, even in this era of supposedly joined up services, and it is particularly brought to the fore with looked after children and others already known to social services.

In working through the three phases of the project, the team debated this insular approach and the neo-liberal flavour of English educational policy of individual (market) freedoms and limited intervention to prevent social ills. We also reflected on far higher rates of imprisonment for young offenders, though less than the USA rate, higher levels of child poverty, still over 15 per cent in the UK in 2009 compared with under 10 per cent for France and most mainland European countries, and the bottom ranking on child well-being reported by UNICEF (2007).

The team also discussed the locating of blame and the fact that, recommended at national level and implemented at school level, we have *discipline* and *behaviour* policies but not *relationship* policies. The first two locate the blame and responsibility with the child – who has the discipline or behaviour problem; to talk of relationships is to share responsibility with the adults and the institution.

It is worth noting at the outset the current limited targeting of advice and guidance: many books are published which focus mainly on the management of behaviour in the school and classroom (Ellis and Tod, 2009; Hallam and Rogers, 2008; Rogers, 2004); likewise, the DCSF material on Behaviour4 Learning individualises the problem through its National Strategies (DCSF, 2008d; 2008d). Good though it is, this material reduces the problem to the level of the teacher in the classroom. This study confirms other levels for action and shows the work, orchestrated by the LA, which has been successful in bringing down exclusions.

As conditions change, so strategic thinking and organisation will need to respond. The DfE white paper, *The Importance of Teaching*, promised a simplification of what was becoming, under the previous administration, an increasingly complex and regulated situation, too often abused by omission and delay. The white paper states that, 'Schools will be free to exclude pupils, but they will then be responsible for finding and funding alternative provision themselves' (DfE 2010, para3.38). Labour's Behaviour and Attendance Partnerships hardly operated meaningfully and the plan to make them mandatory from September 2010 was abandoned by the new government. However, in the spirit of localism and opening up the market, collaborations between schools were vaguely favoured and new providers of alternative educational provision encouraged. Arrangements piloted and set in place by the coalition government may bring exclusions down still further rather than causing a feared return to the levels of exclusion that prevailed when the conservative government left power in 1997.

Finally, this book sets out to show decision-makers at a number of levels what works, or what some LAs have made work, in reducing the need to use exclusions as a way of dealing with unacceptable behaviour. The next chapter gives an account of how the work was carried out. Chapter 3 deals firstly with the successes of low excluding areas enquiring through focused visits how they had done it and how they had maintained low exclusions. Chapter 4 is the core of the book and is about working with five high excluding LAs and examining how they could move to a position of fewer exclusions and certainly back nearer the national average from their starting exclusion position in the top quartile of 150 LAs. Chapter 5 reports the outcomes in terms of reductions in exclusion rates, permanent and fixed period and chapter 6 draws the arguments together and sets out implications for the various stake-holder groups from the DfE to schools and clusters of schools. Chapter 7 gives a more specific inclusion and action plan for LAs. The ultimate goal of the book is to move the emphasis in discussion of exclusion and behaviour from individual teachers and their classes and even individual schools and their ethos and leadership to a sense of community responsibility to make provi-sion suitable to meet the needs of the full range of young people which schools are designed to serve. This is community based inclusion, localism at its best.

2

Methods of enquiring and working

Following a review of national exclusion data and an examination of the situation in three low excluding LAs and Scotland, the project aimed to support five high excluding LAs to identify proactively how they could reduce the number of exclusions by local effort and commitment rather than reactively responding to nationally driven initiatives and pressure or external targets. The project was comprised of three phases.

Phase one: examining national data (England), contacts with Scotland and visiting three low excluding LAs in England

The project began with an analysis of existing national information and data sets. It also identified three low excluding LAs from DfES 2003/04 figures to determine characteristics of good practice in reducing exclusion rates in the current policy environment. This led to the production of instruments and guidance to be used with the five high excluding LAs.

The team collated latest national data on the variation in permanent exclusions across LAs, examining the relationship of this variation to funding, measures of multiple deprivation, allocation of resources and the capacity in the statutory and voluntary sectors to address need and engage in preventative work. Along with providing a valuable picture of the above factors in relation to exclusion, it pointed to specific factors operating in some areas (eg ethnic composition) and provided intelligence on the consistency and changes in exclusion rates in different school types (primary, secondary, special).

Local authority data were marshalled covering census data on all aspects of the population including housing tenure, qualification levels of the population, economic activity (employment), ethnicity, socio-economic status, income, deprivation, GCSE results, key stage results, youth crime offences, SEN, free school meals, looked after children and PRUs. These data were also put together for the five high excluding local authorities. In addition to this, it became evident that school level finance data would be important as schools received varying amounts which were related to deprivation. This prompted speculation about whether the funding was spent on countering economic disadvantage as intended.

In the low excluding LAs, to update understanding of current best practice, 17 interviews were conducted with key LA personnel, as shown in Table 2.1 below. In Scotland, where exclusions are managed differently, a number of key contacts were made, mostly with academics; documentation and further information were gained and fruitful discussions were arranged via email and telephone. From this series of visits, it was possible to develop the *needs assessment and audit of assets tool* to take forward into a sample of five high excluding LAs.

Local Authority	Schools & PRUs	Statutory Services	Voluntary & Community	Pupils	Parents
LA A	3	2	0	0	0
LA B	1	3	2	0	0
LA C	3	2	1	0	0

Table 2.1: Interviews in three low excluding LAs

In each of the three English low excluding LAs, through the systematic accumulation of publicly available background data and interviews, a file was generated on factors and provision associated with exclusion and the management of excluded children. The file included LAs' educational statistics as well as deprivation, crime and employment rates. In each LA, during the course of a one day visit, discussions were held with the individual in charge of exclusions and locally held statistics were examined. Visits to each of the LAs included seeking feedback from samples of teachers and headteachers about promoting inclusion and the consequences, as well as the training and support that has been available (adequacy, quality, appropriateness). The discussions with the low excluding LAs also consolidated existing knowledge and enabled good practice to be identified that would be applied to other LA settings.

Phase two: needs assessment, auditing assets and working with five high excluding LAs

The core of the project was working with five LAs, of different sizes and characters, experiencing high rates of exclusion from schools taking forward the lessons learnt from phase one. This phase took the form of working alongside LAs and key stakeholders including LA officers and members, teachers and other professionals such as Connexions and YOS, voluntary and community organisations and young people and their parents and carers. The goal was to help the LA and schools use alternatives to exclusion and to co-ordinate cross-LA services to address the needs of children and families where there was a risk of the child being excluded from school. The five LAs which agreed to participate in the project are not named.

At the outset, a meeting was convened in each of the LAs with key players and representatives from stakeholder groups with a necessary focus on inviting those individuals who have the power to implement change and disseminate or report back on measures and their effectiveness. These individuals also acted as gatekeepers to other members of their organisation or professional location. The stakeholders were drawn from across disciplines and professional locations including the LA, YOS team, Connexions, local teacher association, VCS etc. The first meeting established the roles and responsibilities of each stakeholder in the development project including that of project staff. It was intended that this group would meet four times throughout the duration of the project to reflect on measures taken from each of the different perspectives, their relative success and next actions.

Following the first meeting of the stakeholder group in each LA, the team carried out a needs assessment documenting the current strategic and practical steps implemented by the LAs to address disaffection and exclusions and audited local provision and resources that could be drawn upon to reduce the level of exclusions. This involved interviews and consultation with a wide range of individuals and groups as set out in Table 2.2 on page 12. Data were collected from 126 people in total.

Access to all groups was negotiated through the LA. In the case of children and families, confidentiality was assured. There was the encouragement for LA personnel to engage in convening further focus groups and consultations using the same methods in order to enhance the data set, but this did not take place. The analysis detailed the current situation on exclusions in each of the local areas and was reported back to the stakeholder group for discussion and any necessary clarification.

Local Authority	Elected member	Schools & PRUs	LA Officers & Statutory Services	Voluntary & Community	Pupils	Parents
LA 1 large metropolitan		6	10	2	7	3
LA 2 small unitary	1	7	11	2	8	3
LA 3 small unitary	1	7	10	1	0	0
LA 4 London borough	1	6	8	1	3	2
LA 5 large county		8	9	2	5	2
Totals	3	34	48	8	23	10

Table 2.2: Interviews and contacts with high excluding LAs

A crucial element to establishing exactly what was best practice, and a commitment of the project, was listening to the young people and their families who had actually experienced exclusion and giving their experiences due weight in the consideration of alternatives and further developments.

Phase three: Consolidating, collective workshop and reporting

A project meeting was convened in March 2008 for all five of the high excluding LAs and representatives of two of the three low excluding LAs available on the day. This was attended by key stakeholders to share findings and discuss successes, failures and further developments. Calculations were made about the number of young people who would directly benefit from their LA's participation in this project based on the LAs' permanent and fixed term exclusion rates from 2003/04 compared with 2007/08. The estimate was that in the five high excluding LAs 430 fewer young people would be permanently excluded and nearly 4,000 fewer instances of fixed period exclusions would occur. Data available in Autumn 2008 for the full 2007/08 year allowed calculations of the degree of success in reducing permanent and fixed term exclusions. Table 2.4 sets out the objectives and performance indicators of the project.

Table 2.4 below gives the number of young people who, it was calculated at the outset, would directly benefit from their LA's participation in this project if the project were optimally successful. The figures are based on the LAs' permanent and fixed term exclusion rates from 2003/04. The goal was that 430 fewer young people would be permanently excluded and that instances of fixed period exclusions would be reduced by over 4,000.

Objective	Performance indicator
1. Reductions in exclusion within the five LAs in Year 1 and Year 2, compared with the 2003/04 baseline	50% reduction in permanent exclusions; 30% reduction in fixed term exclusions (July 2008).
2. Better provision, higher achievement levels and greater inclusion for at risk young people.	Fewer young people out of education or on the 'hard to place' list (20% reduction – July 2008).
3. A fuller understanding at local level of the forces behind high levels of exclusion and the needs of at-risk young people and their families who may be subject to exclusion.	LA officers and stakeholders registering their greater understanding. Young people and their families feeling that their needs are being better heard, understood and met.
4. Processes and tools tailored to their context to tackle exclusions.	LA officers and stakeholders acknowledging appreciation of the tools.
5. Practical recommendations on managing pupils at risk of exclusion using multi-agency approaches including the VCS and operating with supportive and restorative principles.	Recommendations and guidance produced.
6. Criteria of good practice in the management of exclusions.	Criteria produced.
7. A fully documented account of the developmental work with the five action sites, support documentation, action planning.	Documented account produced.

Table 2.3: Objectives and performance indicators

LA	No. of permanent exclusions 2003/04	Potential No. of young people directly benefiting (50% reduction)	No. of pupils with at least 1 fixed period exclusion	Potential No. of young people directly benefiting (30% reduction)
LA 1	330	165	5,462	1639
LA 2	50	25	1,329	399
LA 3	40	20	600	180
LA 4	110	55	1,067	320
LA 5	330	165	7,714	2314
Total	**860**	**430**	**16,172**	**4,852**

Table 2.4: Permanent and fixed period exclusions and reduction targets for 2007/08 in the five high excluding LAs

Setting this example could result in the principles and practices being dis-seminated to many other LAs, meaning that several thousand fewer children are permanently excluded and tens of thousands fewer receive fixed term exclusions. Good LA practice suggests that they will monitor substitute provi-sion to see that it is appropriate and beneficial and that attendance is ade-quate.

The impact of the project was evaluated in the short term by the team and stakeholder partners in the individual LAs (Spring, 2008). The immediate impact of the project was determined via an examination of exclusion figures as the project neared its end and a discussion within the final LA stakeholder groups' meetings regarding their perceptions of impact and any accompany-ing evidence. Exclusion figures for the complete 2007/08 school year were only available from the LAs in September 2008.

Reductions in exclusions were suggested as key performance indicators for the end of the 2007/08 academic year; we hoped to find, and have recorded, changes evident in the phase 3 period and beyond (see Chapter 5).

3

Three local authorities achieving and maintaining low exclusions

Introduction

What the team learned from visiting three low excluding local authorities and making contact with officers and researchers in Scotland confirmed the importance of:

■ robust relationships between the LA and schools

■ supported development of broadened schools, managed transfer and alternative curriculum

■ the cost effectiveness and minimising damage that results from alternatives to exclusion.

In addition, the importance of political backing and the seniority of officers dealing with behaviour and exclusions who could 'do business' with head-teachers and other local authority officers and had some leverage on LA finances.

Local Authority	2001-02	2002-03	2003-04	2004-05	2005-06	2006-07
LA A	0.04	0.02	0.04	0.03	0.04	0.04
LA B	0.19	0.19	0.14	0.00	0.00	0.00
LA C	0.03	0.03	0.02	0.04	0.03	0.03
National Average	0.12	0.13	0.13	0.12	0.12	0.12

Table 3.1: Percentage of the school population permanently excluded

Table 3.1 indicates how two low excluding LAs had a long record of low rates and the third appeared to cut permanent exclusions at a stroke. These examples prove that although behaviour is a factor in exclusion, it is not the sole or even the prime factor. The accounts of achieving and maintaining low exclusions given below are very much the local perspective, based on single day visits to the LAs and examination of data and provision.

LAs A, B and C work in different contexts and ways but there are common stances and practices at a certain level of generality.

Local Authority A

The demographics of what is regarded as an affluent London borough are considered deceptive, masking areas of real deprivation that exist amongst general affluence: two estates are amongst the most deprived in the country. A sizeable minority of the school intake, particularly those that go on to be excluded, are from neighbouring boroughs. These pupils reportedly arrive under a cloud, due to schools in other LAs encouraging parents to remove their children from the school while they still have a choice. Taking pupils in from out of borough was seen to limit the options when it came to trying to avoid exclusion, as the home borough may not always be willing to work with the schools.

Reasons for the fall in permanent exclusions

Working relationships between the schools in the LA were said to be very good (possibly due to the small size of the authority). They will sometimes cooperate amongst themselves with managed moves.

There is a united approach, supported and sustained by a regularly convened *Planning and Placement Panel* (PPP) that meets every 3-4 weeks to discuss those pupils thought to be at risk of exclusion. The panel has representative heads and deputies and other strategic partners. The effort is in trying to identify a solution and finding an appropriate placement for the children.

Internal Exclusion places the young person with one of the senior leadership team in a designated place: an office or another room. This is seen by the pupils to be a real punishment and generally preferred by parents, but it requires sufficient staffing and staff with the right training and credibility with whom the young people can carry out their period of internal exclusion. Schools recognise the need to foster a culture where pupils at risk of exclusion feel wanted. The *PRU* is seen as very helpful for time out for Year 7-9 pupils and for managed moves. A revolving door policy is in place.

All schools have signed up to the *Hard to Place protocol*. All schools have sub-scribed to the principle of taking pupils via a managed move even where they are oversubscribed. Managed moves sometimes (not always) take place via the PRU. There needs to be a balance in schools to ensure managed moves work and that a few schools are not left with a disproportionately high number of children with difficult behaviour.

Managed moves avoid a long process of negotiating the exclusion. There is also much use of counselling and support with the parent to help them make the most appropriate choices in the light of their child's needs. In essence, there is a high degree of support that goes alongside both the move and any other exclusion in order to increase the amount of parental engagement with the process and to ensure that the parents understand that their child has been subject to a raft of measures before they reached the a critical point. There is a need to provide a clear indication to children and parents that managed moves are the last chance before exclusion and that the mediating role of the LA is valued.

Alternative curriculum is well developed in LA A. Schools work with Con-nexions for Year 10 and 11 vocational courses by local providers or the college who run sessions one day a week. Knowing that the option is available has prevented a high number of exclusions from Year 9. The college is very expen-sive for the school budget, but schools feel the option is well worth it, keeping the children in education, on the school roll, and helping them to perform, integrate and achieve.

Achieving and maintaining low levels of exclusion
All schools have devolved funding and buy in services provided by the LA as required. All schools buy in Educational Psychologist (EP) time. Time out placements in the PRU are dependent on EP involvement, used by the LA as a measure that the schools have tried to cope with the situation in house. Two schools have a social inclusion worker.

The success is considered to be essentially due to the hard work of schools and supporting services. The Director of Social Inclusion ensures that the process of inclusion is driven by someone who is able to ensure that the part-nership between schools and LAs is strong and efficient. There is a high degree of cooperation amongst schools and between the schools and the LA, initially through the inclusion officer. Partnership working has significant sign-up in schools with the managed moves protocol operating well. Schools and the LA recognise the significance of their relationship with parents and work hard to establish a cooperative partnership with them.

Two PRUs are used mainly for time out provision and to ease transfers in managed moves. Vocational provision is currently taken up by 60-70 pupils and three courses are available at the local college: hair and beauty, sport and motor mechanics. One school contracts with a college in a neighbouring LA and buys into courses there. The usefulness of these courses is appreciated but they do need to be used appropriately.

The LA publishes all schools' exclusion data for all to see. This followed the establishment of the PPP in 2001, with clear terms of reference and a membership of heads/deputies, the assistant director on inclusions, EPs, EWOs, YOT, Connexions and social workers. This flags up the value of multi-agency involvement, which also facilitates the production of a multi-dimensional portrait of the pupil. There is a need to know which other agencies are involved with the pupil. Such information sharing can change the approach to exclusion or a managed move; these steps may be inappropriate if there is currently little stability in their life, and the decision would then be to keep the pupil in school for longer.

The LA coordinates out of school services to provide appropriate support packages for pupils. The LA can organise, for example, pupil support services, youth services, the PRU, YOT, EWS, the inclusion officer and Connexions, and all the negotiation is carried out by the LA.

The cost to schools for avoiding exclusion, in terms of money, energy and time, 'is huge' but the pupils are 'without question' getting a better deal with the current approach. Though considered sustainable, the situation was expected to worsen with the new guidance on providing full-time education for pupils excluded for more than five days; the LA expected to top slice school budgets to provide for this.

Local Authority B

LA B is the only local authority to achieve zero permanent exclusions for two consecutive years. It has 14 Secondary schools, one PRU and lots of alternative provision, called 'Personalised Learning'. There is a positive sense of the LA having a responsibility for making appropriate provision, but only in partnership with the schools.

There is evidence of a widening range of backgrounds amongst those in senior positions in school where these better meet the needs of the young people; two assistant heads in one school were not teacher trained and the Officer for Learner Engagement was from Careers, not teaching, and has done much to broaden the range of alternative provision.

Reasons for the fall in exclusion figures

Exclusion figures have been reduced mostly by the provision of what they call personalised learning (rather than alternative provision). It is greatly supported by a solution-focused approach which has been supported by in-house training. A partnership between the LA, schools and other providers has established collaborative working, essential for appropriate and effective provision.

Monthly meetings are attended by three secondary headteachers, who represent the schools, the Head of Social Inclusion and the Advisory Officer for Learner Engagement. No decision is made by the heads or by the authority – it must be mutually agreed. The council cabinet member for education attends briefings with senior managers every Thursday morning. This establishes a strong connection between education and policy makers. BIP money has undoubtedly helped. They have set up an off-site provision for those who are receiving fixed-term exclusions.

There is a policy for managed moves and hard to place pupils, but the feeling is that managed moves are for one-off actions where, for example, someone is badly hurt in an incident, and not for persistently disruptive pupils. There is an assumption that the latter can, mostly, be maintained with support in their mainstream school.

In two secondary schools and three primary schools in the BIP cluster, nurture groups were established. One school has no facility which they would call an LSU or Inclusion Unit. Instead, there is an 'Academy' and pupils contract to come in. Younger ones can come in if they have an issue. For older pupils, there is a more personalised curriculum in which some come in for just one period a week and some for five or six. Teachers cannot refer or send children there, although they might have wanted to; in other words, it has to be as an outcome of an assessment not an unconsidered reaction by a class teacher. Some children come out and are supported back in mainstream. The LA does a good deal of individual work with parents through the very practical Family Support Service which is based in the school but is not just for the school. Where there is an exclusion, the Parenting Officer will ring the parent and ask if they want support.

Achieving and maintaining low levels of exclusion

In one school, there is the Gateway Programme for Key Stage 4 pupils which has 90 students. They are in a section headed 'Inspiring Minds', where they do project work in Year 9 (20 students). They have different tracks at Key Stage 3, a Nurture Group which is run by a lead behaviour professional. They have jig-saws in these rooms for calm work for the youngsters and also Success Maker on the computer. In one of the groups they have pupils who are weak in both literacy and numeracy; if they are weak in just one they are supported in mainstream.

The Education Support Team for the BIP Group comprises 0.8 of an EP, a clinical psychologist covering three schools, learning mentors, CAMHS and has the intention to establish what good practice in multi-agency working consists of. The LA has its own Multi-agency Prevention Service, which champions a restorative justice approach, but has no policy on permanent exclusion.

An off site facility is shared by two secondary schools and can take up to 15 pupils. Probably 120 pupils pass through each year. It is for incidents in school and is clearly a punishment which pupils must undergo before returning to their school. It is run by a team of non-teachers, BIP funded, and they have experimented with different staffing arrangements. Now there are six Student Support Officers and no-one has the lead; this means that if anyone is away the Unit can continue to function. When numbers are low in the Unit they go into school to meet the pupils with whom they have a continuing support role. This is a commissioning approach to PRU provision, where the LA contracts out its PRU provision to its schools to run them in ways which are best suited to their needs and provision and recognises the related provision in school.

Instead of a confrontational and conflict situation with difficult pupils they have adopted a solution focused approach and have invested in Gilman Training (Hook and Vass, 2000). Training included all ancillary staff, and two staff from every school received intensive training to share at their schools.

They closed the Primary PRU and retrained the staff to provide support in schools for pupils who needed help with their behaviour. The closure saved £330,000 and the money was used for personalised learning and nurture groups. The EP service is now high profile and is renamed the Educational Psychology and Behaviour Service. The authority then felt more confident about relaxing the grip of the National Curriculum, particularly where there are pupil mental heath problems.

The Behaviour and Education Support Team (BEST) works in the eight BIP schools and the Multi-agency Preventative Team covers the rest. Health, the LAC team, Safer Schools, YOT, police and drugs workers are also involved. They do not think of themselves as separate teams and the LA is trying to see itself as a Campus for Learning (with one school uniform across the authority). Termly meetings would include the EPU (Educational Preparation Unit) for between four and twelve pre-school children. More family level work is done, they have expanded the Educational Welfare Service and have two parenting projects working out of two of the secondary schools.

Several pupils each year were referred out of the LA to expensive special school placements. Many were brought back, making a considerable saving. 'It's cheaper to deal with them yourself than to send them to the other side of the country'.

Heads agreed to set a target of zero permanent exclusions in the face of DfES targets. They used four sources of funding: the AWPU plus Band 3 statemented money, money from schools, the pupil retention grant idea and BIP money. Schools expected the LA to produce packages, and they needed a monitoring panel, which three headteachers run, with input from other LA services. There is a moderation panel for placements to ensure that the school has tried all the strategies and done all it can to resolve the problem.

Alternative provision is diverse and engages the pupils in activities with possibilities for qualifications to be gained at the end. For example, one pupil attends two days a week at the Equestrian Centre and three days at the ICT suite in the LA offices, staffed by one teacher and two assistants. Another attends for two days each week at the ICT Centre, two days at the Young Persons Education Centre studying maths and basic skills, and one day at the IT facility called Second Byte.

The Equestrian Centre costs £8 per hour or £42 per day. Pupils study for ASDAN and the British Horse Society Horse Owners Certificate. Approximately nine pupils attend the course during any one week, but with different patterns of attendance. There is a food room in which they study maths (buying tack) and discuss environmental issues (electric fences).They benefit through raised self-esteem and developing social skills. The LA also has access to Study United at a local football league ground. It offers ASDAN and Playing for Success qualifications. It is staffed by two teachers, an assistant, a learning mentor, an ICT specialist and a driver who also does some mentoring. There are eight regular volunteers and they are seeking more. Another off-site centre will cover the rest of the secondary schools. For the 75 places contracted for three years at alternative providers, referred to as independent schools, targets are set in terms of A to C grades.

There is funding for those on the verge of exclusion and courses are offered for a range of pupils, including the CLAIT (basic IT) qualification, an autistic group, GCSE Business studies and ICT in the Community, Leisure and Tourism. It is funded with £25,000 from the LA, £50,000 from the DfES and £50,000 from the football club. The cost to schools is on a sliding scale depending on the level of supervision. The LA and schools nonetheless agree that this is cost effective and a better solution than exclusion or referral to an EBD school outside the authority.

There is confidence that the support needed for many pupils is available and nil exclusions was judged to be 'cost-neutral'. Pupils are getting a better deal, it is sustainable and the collective belief is that 'reacting is not enough'.

Local Authority C

LA C is a small metropolitan borough. It is an area with above average figures for unemployment, single parents and a much higher proportion of residents with no qualifications.

Reasons for the fall in permanent exclusions

In LA C, there is strong political backing for maintaining low exclusions, particularly from the Cabinet Lead Member for Education. It regards itself as a socially inclusive LA. In the late 1990s, a political initiative was launched called the 'Zero Rejection' policy. It was at the time when the LA was required to produce a Behaviour Support Plan and in this it also included plans for Alternative Provision. Added to the Zero Rejection policy was the case work approach in dealing with exclusion, and experience has shown that high quality case workers are of paramount importance.

Schools were won over by the support of the LA, the casework approach and the message that exclusion devalues education and has a damaging effect on the pupil. The guidance and leadership from the LA and the commitment that hard to place pupils come with support were important. Knowing there are professionals who will work closely with the school and give considerable support further consolidated the inclusion message. There is a strong culture of partnership between schools and agencies. LA C has a School Improvement Partnership Board which has on it elected headteachers who meet with the lead managers in the other services. They manage an £18M budget for school improvement and some of this funding is also for social inclusion.

LA C has an Alternative Provision Admission Panel which the Head of Psychology and Behaviour chairs. On the Panel are the heads of the alternative providers and they employ an ex-headteacher colleague to administer it and oil the wheels and also to chair the Secondary School Inclusion Advisory Placement Panel which meets monthly. Six headteachers meet with the admissions team. It makes recommendations to the receiving school and, though its function is advisory, there is pressure that can (and is) brought to bear. LA C has contended with forces which push exclusions up, such as a zero tolerance stance over drugs or weapons. Not all the schools have always been cooperative in taking their share of hard to place pupils. Failing schools are acknowledged as adding to the pressure.

Achieving and maintaining low levels of exclusion

The key to achieving and maintaining low levels of permanent exclusion is to have layers of provision and a team of workers to assign or refer and to monitor progress closely, maximising support in schools and for schools. When a pupil has to take time out from school, work is done to enhance their chances of returning to mainstream education and settling successfully.

The LA is divided into nine areas and each has a School Improvement Partnership (SIP) team. In three of the neediest areas, the SIP is enhanced by a Behaviour and Education Support Team (BEST). Each area has about two secondary and nine primary schools. With the BEST, staffing is multi-agency and numbers about 20. These offer quick response and case working with the most difficult young people, including arranging for alternative placement. EPs are now intimately involved and one coordinates each team. One of the indicators for EPs is the proportion of 'excluded' who are settled within three weeks. The LA was a Phase 1 Behaviour Improvement Project (BIP) authority and used the money to make three of the teams into BESTs, which have become the model for Children and Young People's work and for developments around Every Child Matters.

The solutions available to schools are extensive. In one secondary school, these include an exclusion unit, which has proved very effective since opening in 2004. Very few pupils are referred to the PRU now because early intervention is the norm. Alternative curricula are extensively used. Two teachers operate a community classroom, where they have specialist school status for ICT, and use resources from it. Staff training is used for behaviour management.

Multi-agency working across the authority is considered to be 'very, very good in this LA'. There are numerous agencies and out of school provision options to support schools which are arranged and monitored by the SIPS team. They include:

- Local colleges providing vocational courses
- Notschool.net, an online national development with 60 places
- Holistic Approaches Centre, takes 15 pupils
- Key team for PCT-SS-Ed, takes 20 pupils
- NACRO for KS3 and 4, three or two days a week for six weeks, by referral
- Groundwork for KS3 and 4, an outdoor education centre, but expensive
- Connexions, a carers club
- Base 25, an anger management group
- YWCA, for one afternoon a week
- League Football Club, sports leadership for one afternoon a week
- Re-Entry, a charity for six pupils for three days a week. They have links with a regeneration officer, the police, fire service and street wardens. They also attend neighbourhood meetings which serves as a good link with the community
- Spurgeons, a charity working with pupils and parents on issues such as self esteem and anger management
- Work experience
- COPE 14-19, Pathfinder work, Explorer courses.

The costs are significant and the LA is overspent on alternative provision. Finance will be found because this is a key factor in the LA's drive for inclusion. Schools have agreed to be top sliced by £250K for one of the charity providers which works with behaviourally challenging pupils. Pupils are undoubtedly getting a better deal, although there were no figures on achievement to scrutinise at that time. There is conviction that the current way of working is sustainable but also a recognised need for a 'social inclusion audit' to know what schools have already got, what the LA puts in and what training is needed.

Scotland

Our enquiries amongst colleagues in Scotland confirmed the levers for reducing exclusion. Statistics published by the Scottish government for 2007/08 show big reductions in exclusions from schools in 2007/08. Ninety nine per cent of exclusions were temporary, lasting for an average of three days. There were just 164 permanent exclusions, where pupils are 'removed from the register of the school'. It is the lowest figure this century. If Scotland permanently excluded at the same rate as England, the figure would be nearly 1,000.

The Schools Minister, Maureen Watt (2009), said strategies to manage pupil behaviour such as the use of nurture groups, pupil support bases, college and vocational placements, and personal and social development programmes were at the root of the reduction. She states that:

> The significant drop in exclusions is a clear indication that the range of approaches and provision available within and beyond school is working. Schools and local authorities are using a wide range of provisions to reduce exclusions, with a focus on intervening early to stop problem situations before they develop into serious issues.

The national support, local authority interventions, the culture and commitment of schools and community expectations of inclusive schooling appear to form a consolidated wave of support for finding ways to support young people through their education, with minimal recourse to punitive responses.

It should also be noted that the unique Children's Hearing system is less formal and more care-oriented than procedures for young people in trouble with the law which are in place for young people in England. In 1971, the Children's Hearings took over from the courts responsibility for children under 16. The reports of the Scottish Children's Hearings over the years have been enviably positive.

What can be learnt from the low excluding LAs?
From these three visits and an examination of Scottish procedures, the following interim conclusions were recorded and taken on to the main part of the project.

Powerfully driven from within education
All of the local authorities appeared to have a person driving for lower exclusions. These officers were fairly high in the hierarchy and had clout. They could work effectively on two fronts: firstly, they could sit at the same table as headteachers and confront them whilst also being able to negotiate provision and alternatives to exclusion; secondly, within the local authority they were able to re-direct resources and create sustainable and costed facilities to meet the needs of young people at risk of exclusion. Headteachers see that the person they were dealing with could deliver. A sense of real bargaining could take place, trust was established and an ongoing dialogue could be maintained.

Political backing

In all three local authorities there was backing from key elected members. Councillors took an interest in the workings of the system and in one LA the cabinet member for Education was involved in weekly discussions on a range of issues which might include inclusion.

Schools on board

It was evident from discussions with headteachers that they had conditionally signed up to the nil or low exclusions approach. There was even a sense of pride in that it allowed them to proceed in ways which were less punitive than they knew exclusions to be. However, their compliance with the locally agreed low exclusions policy was conditional on their receiving support in schools and on being able to reach help within the local authority quickly and being able to have a child removed to another place if matters became intolerable.

With some additional resources, schools also took on a greater responsibility for managing young people who found it difficult to adjust to normal behaviour in classrooms. Some had units, others had multiple layers of provision and still others had part time curricular or dual registration in order to maintain the young person in education.

Alternative provision

As well as Pupil Referral Units, local authorities had additional sorts of provision for education other than at school. Small local authorities did not need a long list of alternative provision and what was available was generally listed, brokered and quality assured by local authority personnel. It was possible to allocate a young person to a range of provision whilst still being attached to the school roll with the prospect that they may go back should matters improve. In one local authority a young person might spend three mornings a week at the equestrian centre, three afternoons a week at basic skills and other days with youth and community or on a vocational placement. The worry about quality being high enough and attendance being good enough are generally covered by the authorities which have recognised the usefulness of good provision and its superiority to standard PRU placements.

Managed moves

In the three local authorities, managed moves were a supporting part of the inclusion policy. Officers weighed the evidence about whether a supported fresh start would work or whether it should be accepted that if the child could not make it at one school why they should be able to make it at another. Where there has been a specific breakdown of relationships, due perhaps to violence or drugs, managed moves were organised. This was particularly promoted for those excluded for out of character, one off incidents.

Multi-agency teams

All three LAs had multi-agency teams which attempted to respond quickly to calls from schools. They played support and problem-solving roles with challenging pupils but also acted as mediators with parents and other agencies which might pay a role. BIP and BEST funding had been used to good effect in these LAs to innovate – or in some cases reinvent – behaviour support teams, new configurations of professionals and new management arrangements.

Achieving and sustaining low exclusion rates

In all three LAs, it was evident that there was considerable vigilance and continuing willingness to adapt provision. This was always in co-ordination with the schools. The creation of a low exclusion ethos needs to be driven at the level of values and principles but also sold on the levels of finance and service effectiveness. The commitment to low exclusions needs to be marshalled at the levels of local government members, senior education (now Children's Services) officers and headteachers. In addition, this must involve the commitment of resources, sometimes not new resources but re-allocated resources, so that it is clear to everyone that schools can develop their own facilities for challenging youngsters This can involve additional staff who work with these youngsters inside and outside the school and appropriate alternative provision which is available, accessible and can be organised with the local authority help.

4
Working with five high excluding local authorities

Introduction

Phase two of the work in each of the five partner high excluding LAs began with a stakeholders' group meeting convened by the LA. The team then generated lists of professionals to be interviewed and the team interviewed senior staff in 34 schools, 48 officers and other professionals working in statutory organisations and three local politicians. Interviews were also conducted with 23 young people and 10 parents.

The action phase of the project comprised further more focused enquiries such as into why primary exclusions had increased and how inclusion units in schools were functioning. Attempts to work more directly with schools or with a specific element of the exclusion story proved to be difficult and our function was usually to advise the local authority's strategy group and to engage in further information gathering and feedback.

Stakeholder group meetings

It was intended that the stakeholder group would contain a range of professionals and representation from the voluntary and community sector. It was hoped that headteachers would also be centrally involved and that the group would number around 12. In the event few headteachers took part. Three or four meetings were held with the stakeholder group over the course of the project, convened by the senior officer who had oversight of exclusions.

As well as being an internal source of information and guidance it was also important that the stakeholder group members be advocates for the way forward. It was hoped that they would engage with us in gathering information but they only provided data they already held.

A considerable quantity of data had been gathered from the Web. The LA provided specific information on their own population, characteristics of those excluded pupils and, later, school finance data. It was possible to identify the services involved, most obviously statutory services, with voluntary and community sector projects seeming peripheral – however promoted and well intentioned they were.

In presenting data to the stakeholder group the intention was to show how the LA compared with the three low excluding authorities visited, with the national average and with its statistical neighbours.

The first meeting also examined LA statistics on exclusion by school, sector and pupil characteristics. It examined exclusion rates over time, identified emerging issues and portrayed graphically the difference between permanent exclusions at the secondary school level compared with the rate for the country as a whole. Showing the trend over a number of years emphasised the sustained nature of the problem. In one LA, to convey the point that some interventions were not working as intended, the feedback to the stakeholder group concentrated on the BIP schools (schools with significant additional funding to address behaviour) and their continued higher level exclusions.

Questions were asked about: numbers out of school and in PRUs and reintegration rates; the cost of a PRU place; out of school resources to support inclusion; and nationally funded groups operating locally. Enquiries were also made about the relationship between schools and the local authority, its importance and the degree of respect and trust.

The extensive data gathered from the internet (listed in Box 1) covered the full range of relevant data from the 2001 census, Index of Multiple Deprivation 2004 and DfES data available on the internet. These data were of interest in relation to possible or claimed reasons for higher rates of exclusion. For the most part, these data did not offer credible explanations for higher rates of exclusion in an LA.

From the LA, specific information was needed on their own population. These data requested are set out in Box 2. We were particularly interested in the exclusion data by school and the characteristics of those excluded either permanently or for a fixed period. Such information would help with discussions about targeting interventions to prevent further exclusions. As time went on, we became more interested in the finance data (Box 2, e and h). Schools would make claims about what they could or could not afford. Some schools received considerably more than others in funding per pupil and

Box1: Local Authority Profile

1. census overview (population etc)
2. ethnicity
3. social-economic status
4. economic activity
5. income support claimants
6. jobseekers' allowance claimants
7. deprivation
8. household composition
9. dependent children
10. Special Educational Needs and free school meals entitlement
11. qualifications
12. GCSE results
13. KS1
14. KS2
15. KS3
16. health
17. criminal offences
18. Pupil Referral Units
19. secondary schools information
20. statistical neighbour data

some schools had reserves. We were able to identify the services which schools used, though voluntary and community sector projects seemed largely peripheral – however well intentioned they were.

Box 3 lists the key measures found to be working in the low excluding local authorities and these were presented to the stakeholder groups. In that the secondary schools exclude over 80 per cent of all those excluded, nurture groups at Year 7, or some similar supportive experience, appeared to be important. So also was the availability of alternative provision for those at Key Stage 4. It appeared that the 'big beasts' in the LA needed to be playing a lead role, to do business with the headteachers, to bring down exclusions. Equally strategic staff and elected members needed to play a part.

We presented the LA with stimulus data, including tables and graphs. The purpose was to undermine the argument that special conditions pertained in this LA and that lower rates could not be achieved. It was intended to confront the position taken that it is all about the levels of pupil problem behaviour and that permanent exclusion in the LA is always a last resort!

Box 2: Data requested for preliminary analysis

A. Young People and School Data

a) school lists for 2005/06 with permanent exclusion numbers for the last three years.

b) school lists for 2005/06 with fixed period exclusion incidents for the last three years (with total days lost)

c) Data by school listing exclusions by year group, gender, ethnicity, LAC, FSM status and SEN status for both permanent and fixed period exclusions

d) PRU provision/roll with data as above on individuals with reintegration rates

e) Cost of PRU place

f) Attainment and crime outcomes for Y11 pupils excluded 2005/06

g) Table of reasons for exclusion

h) Finance for each school showing AWPU and all the other additions to school budget

i) Full list of alternative education providers with numbers of places, age range, average on roll and cost per place

j) School list with attainment levels (% level 4 at KS2; % A*-C grades at KS4)

B. Services Data in relation to social inclusion in education

BIP/ BEST / Behaviour Support Team staffing

Alternative Education providers with numbers of YP (2005/06)

FE college role in providing alternative education

Social Services projects/involvement

Child and Adolescent Mental Health Services projects/involvement

Voluntary and Community Sector projects/involvement

C. Specific issues given (by some) as reasons for high exclusions

eg transient population/ out of area pupils/ poverty levels/ day six rule

Box 3: Low excluder strategies: multiple measures both preventative and intervention focused

- Use of Year 7 support/nurture groups

- Availability of extended curriculum for Years 10 -11

- Multi-agency support teams (inc. use of BEST and BIP)

- Use of and role (status) of EP

- Practice of internal exclusions and off-site FT exclusions

- Partnership working between schools

- Family involvement and the provision of holistic support

- Use of skilled staff

- Involvement of strategic personnel from LA and elected members

Low excluding LA	No. of perm exc 2004/5	% of school pop.	No. of fixed term exc 2004/05	% of school pop.
LA A	10	0.03%	700	3.28%
LA B	0	0.0%	1,940	7.73%
LA C	20	0.04%	1,260	3.11%
LA 2	360	0.21%	8,300	4.74%
Nat. Av		0.12%		5.12%

Table 4.1: Findings from three low excluding LAs: data profile with LA 2 and national figures

In presenting data to the stakeholder group, we sought to show how the LA compared with the three low excluding authorities visited – which were named to them on a power point slide. Table 4.1 shows LA 2's exclusions in comparison with the low excluders and the national average; while permanent exclusions are well above the national average, LA 2 actually performs better for fixed period exclusions and, indeed, has a lower rate than low excluding LA B's fixed period exclusions.

It was also possible to compare the local authority's exclusion rate with its statistical neighbours. Table 4.2 shows that LA 2 was considerably higher in its exclusion rate than most of the other statistical neighbour LAs. Two were in fact higher than LA 2; one of these had been given the opportunity to join the

LA	% of the total school population permanently excluded (2003/04)
LA m	0.20
LA n	0.09
LA o	0.10
LA p	0.09
LA q	0.02
LA r	0.13
LA s	0.14
LA t	0.25
LA u	0.18
LA v	0.01
LA 2	0.19

Table 4.2: Permanent exclusions 2003/04, LA 2 and statistical neighbours

---

Box 4: Exclusion facts LA 3

Exclusion facts – primary

Primary permanent exclusions at national average of 0.03% (but 3 up to 5 in 05/06)
☐ 3 separate schools
FT exclusions at 61 instances and a rate of 0.69% of the school population (down to 57 in 05/06)
☐ Lower than the national average of 1.04%
☐ One school accounts for 44% of FT exclusions
Possibility of nil exclusions?

Exclusion facts – secondary

Permanent exclusions at 40 instances and a rate of 0.66% of the school population (down to 24 in 05/06 and rate of 0.39%)
☐ Higher than the national average of 0.24%
☐ One school accounts for 38% of permanent exclusions (50% in 05/06)
FT exclusions at 611 instances and a rate of 10.02% of the school population (up to 632 in 05/06)
☐ Slightly higher than the national average rate of 9.94%
☐ Three schools account for 73% of FT exclusions (71% in 05/06)

---

project but had felt 'the time is not right'. The fact that LA q and LA v score so low is a startling contrast to the permanent exclusion rate for LA 2 in 2003/04.

We also presented some interpretations and anomalies in the local data. Box 4 indicates the data on LA 3, which we fed back to their first stakeholder meeting. Primary school exclusions numbers are fairly low in all the local authorities, even if higher than the national average, but it is possible to point to the possibility of nil exclusions. For secondary exclusions we emphasised the higher rates in these local authorities and also the concentration of exclusions in a small number of schools. In LA 3, one of the six secondary schools excluded 38 per cent and then 50 per cent of all of the permanent exclusions. Three of the six schools accounted for 73 per cent of fixed term exclusions.

Figure 4.1 portrayed graphically the difference between permanent exclusions at the secondary school level for LA 3 compared with the rate for the country as a whole. Showing the trend over a number of years also emphasised the sustained nature of the problem.

For LA 4, a bar graph (Figure 4.2) presenting permanent exclusions year by year, showed how that local authority had secondary school exclusions at a rate that was, for most years, more than double the national rate.

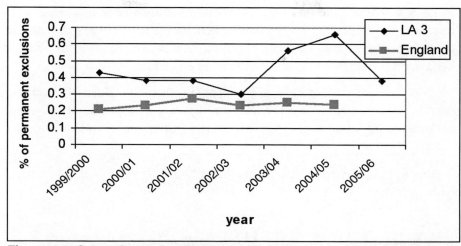

Figure 4.1: Secondary school permanent exclusions – LA3 and England – 1999-2005/6

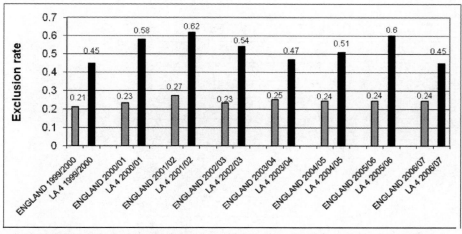

Figure 4.2: Secondary school permanent exclusions nationally and in LA 4 – 1999-2006

Box 5 presented the reasons for exclusion and provided a basis for discussion about the manageability of pupils displaying these challenging behaviours. For LA 1, disruption and physical abuse to pupils (fighting) were the top reasons for exclusions. In LA 3 verbal abuse of staff and persistent disruptive behaviour were the top 'offences'. Possession of a weapon – 12.8 per cent in LA 1 – is a serious worry, but this is not listed at all for LA 3. Drug and alcohol related offences remain a constant minority of about 5 per cent of exclusions and may need to be addressed in particular ways.

In LA 4, to convey the point that some interventions were not working as intended, the feedback (Box 6) to the stakeholder group concentrated on the eight BIP schools (schools with significant additional funding to address behaviour) and their continued higher level exclusions.

We posed a number of questions (Box 8) arising from the data on LA 5, many of which were similar across the LAs. For instance, we asked about numbers of pupils out of school and in PRUs and reintegration rates (3 and 4); the cost

Box 5: Reason for exclusion – LA 1

	%
Arson	1.38%
Bullying – physical	1.03%
Defiance	8.97%
Continued disruption – lessons	4.14%
Continued disruption – school	23.10%
Drug dealing and/or possession	4.48%
Extortion	0.3%
Physical abuse to others	0.3%
Physical abuse to pupils	15.2%
Physical abuse to staff	8.3%
Physical abuse with a weapon	1.7%
Sexually inappropriate behaviour to pupils	2.8%
Sexually inappropriate behaviour to staff	0.7%
Theft	2.1%
Threatening behaviour	6.6%
Vandalism	0.7%
Verbal abuse to staff	5.5%
Possession of a weapon	12.8%

Box 6: Points for discussion – LA 4 secondary exclusions

- 2005/06 secondary permanent exclusions 110 (0.51%) (national secondary rate 0.24%)
- 8 BIP schools out of 21 excluded 40 out of 96 pupils in 2004/05 (42%) and 65 out of 110 in 2005/06 (59%)
- In BIP schools, exclusion rate rose from 0.54 per cent to 0.88 per cent from 2004/05 to 2005/06
- 2 non-BIP schools are high excluders but their exclusions fell slightly over the 2 years

of a PRU place was of interest because it took money that could be used in other ways. We asked about the out of school resources to support inclusion – faith or ethnic groups, community groups, nationally funded groups operating locally. We asked about the relationship between schools and the local authority, how important it was, whether it was robust and whether it was a relationship characterised by respect and trust.

Box 7: Issues LA 5

1. Why the difference between primary and secondary school exclusion rates in comparison with national averages?
2. Why the increasing secondary FT exclusions and high permanents?
3. Why the high numbers out of school and in PRUs?
4. What are the reintegration rates?
5. PRU places are expensive – not just in LA 5; is an increase in this capacity the way to go?
6. What out-of-school resources are there to support inclusion? (from the LA? from other sources?)
7. Has LA 5 identified sufficient alternative providers?
8. What is the relationship between schools and the LA?
9. How can existing funding be used to support school-focused inclusion?
10. How big is the BIP budget and is it used effectively?

The action which followed in each LA was to begin with investigations. These began with interviews with a wide range of people, followed by small scale support initiatives. In the event, the small scale support initiatives did not occur but were replaced by further, more focused enquiries.

Assessment of need and audit of assets in five high excluding local authorities

The needs assessment comprised a systematic exploration of each LA's exclusion policy, practice and relationships and the extent and nature of the needs of the target population. The rationale was that this would determine the range and capacity of services required to meet needs better and help plan and implement services more effectively.

The audit of assets was conducted at the same time, using data gathered from the same interviewees. It was to involve a thorough examination, description and listing of assets and services relating to exclusions. This was intended to lead to a greater awareness and better use of services available to support reduced exclusions across statutory services and VCS, to identify any gaps in provision and areas for multi-agency working. The proposals the project would return with, tailored to each LA, would arise from in-depth discussions and data collection with service providers, users and related stakeholders.

The sections which follow focus on the five high excluding LAs in turn, their exclusion profile and initiatives and policies to reduce exclusion. Two final sections deal with the views of pupils who have been excluded and their parents and school finance and its relationship to measures of deprivation in the school intake.

Accounting for the rates of exclusion and developments in the five high excluding LAs

The five LAs analysed and reported on in the following pages are anonymised. It should be noted that the reports are historical and ongoing contacts with LA officers indicate that the commitment and work continues. Where there have been reductions, it is difficult for this project to take credit; its role may have been as another agent prompting thinking and action. The experience of the project confirmed the power and influence of the LA and it is to their credit, and their schools, where rates of exclusion have been reduced.

Local authority 1 (LA 1)

Preliminary analysis

LA 1 is a large urban authority with around 100 secondary schools and 300 primary schools. Ethnically diverse and with significant areas of severe deprivation, it has major challenges to deliver an effective, inclusive and high performing system of education. Statistics for 2003/04 indicated that primary school permanent exclusions were marginally higher than national average: 0.05 per cent compared to 0.03 per cent. The permanent exclusion rate for secondary schools of 0.43 per cent of the school population was distinctly higher than the national average of 0.24 per cent. Over a six year period from 2001, permanent exclusions from all the authority's school had been practically at the national average for several years and then rose dramatically above it, falling again to 0.17 per cent in 2005/06, when the national average rate was 0.12 per cent.

There has been an increasing rate of fixed term exclusions at secondary level, rising from a little under the national average to significantly above in the three years to 2005/06.

Reasons for high rates of exclusion

Eight officers from a range of services including BIP, Behaviour Support and Police met with the project team at the first stakeholder meeting. A round table discussion was held to determine the primary causes of exclusions in LA 1, and the current responses. The results are set out below in Table 4.3.

Causes	Responses
Unsupported transitions	School Cluster arrangements
Lack of support in primary and any support that has been provided not picked up in secondary	Fresh Start programme
	Family involvement
Diverse routes in variety of secondary school	
Bullying, violent behaviour	Roehampton research to provide information for new city-wide anti-bullying strategy
Lack of school 'community'; linked to travel to school factors	
Continued disruption in lessons	BIP funding
	KS4 alternative provision – but this is not used enough
No tradition of managed moves	Now used and high rate of success reported
Lack of collaborative working	Holistic working with family
Size of LA an issue?	
Low tolerance by some school staff around 'problem' behaviour and issues around continuity in discipline	Letter from Director of LA to schools regarding high exclusion rate
Amount of support in school	
Impact of national agenda	
Leadership and management eg the philosophy of heads towards exclusions	
SEN identified but needs not promptly met as provision not available	
Resources: excluded young people can access specialist support	
Violence – particular problem around weapons. Issue around weapons – how to deal with the issue in school	– Partnership between education and police/YOT — early intervention in schools by police
Continuity in staffing in schools and issues around staff fatigue	
Raising of stakes when pupils reach secondary level eg targets.	Solution sought at the local authority council cabinet level
Perverse incentives to exclude	
Awareness of Alternative Education options by secondary heads and special needs department is low (these options are not accessible to Yr 9)	There is an Alternative Education directory, available since 2004. Providers are quality controlled

Table 4.3: Perceived causes of exclusion and reported responses

At the political level, it is said that reducing exclusions is a high priority, but, as an LA officer said, 'we have a vast range of need'. Current restructuring and reorganisation may help but there has been 'inertia and lack of leadership, courage, confidence' (ie at senior officer and member levels).

LA 1 has encouraged headteachers to follow the procedures for exclusion – including recording fixed term exclusions. This has led to a rise in numbers recorded. When permanent exclusions were at their lowest in LA 1, the impact was reportedly seen elsewhere, eg. in a rise of young people not in school, suggesting that driving down exclusions results in unofficial exclusion.

Assets available
Discussion at the first stakeholder meeting and subsequent interviews indicated a range of assets available to support inclusion. As well as a list of alternative education providers and involvement from some charities there were many initiatives, most originated by the LA.

- Fair access sharing panels in the six areas coming into effect in September 2007, with two pilots underway before this

- Twelve full-time police officers operate in schools – four in BIP schools. The budget for behavioural support services has not kept pace with new legislation. New resources are coming from different pathways but are not always coordinated or working together to achieve similar goals – this is not helped by a lack of communication

- Some young people are reluctant to leave the PRU because of the high standard of care they receive

- There has been a correlation between a fall in exclusions at primary level and the LA marketing its services:

  - services have been provided on a fast response, flexible and graduated basis

  - primary services are working with a similar number of pupils but before they have been excluded

  - the LA is on the way to nil exclusions at primary level but the scale is so much bigger at secondary level and a much larger resource is required

  - strategies are used in Year 6 that are not sustainable in Year 7 partly due to the mobility of the school population

- the LA is rolling out the SEAL programme at primary level. It is currently in the third year and reaching half of all primary schools

■ One of the pilot panels for exclusions has offered encouraging results for secondary level

■ Good rate of reintegration except at KS 4 where pupils are offered alternative curriculum programmes

■ In 2002/03 national targets and fines for exclusions were removed and there was a reintroduction a simpler system of money following the pupil – prior to this schools were not accurately recording exclusions, but they are now

■ The impact of the ECM agenda working to improve communication and ownership

■ Sharing panels are in operation looking at admissions for hard to place young people. These were designed to lower exclusion rates but need greater capacity to respond to issues raised by panel eg postcode (deprivation) issues and the need to keep some young people local rather than having a distant school place offered.

What is working

LA 1 is an authority which strives to organise its own provision for the full range of its pupils. Amongst the initiatives operating are the following:

■ Managed moves, for which it was said the LA had no tradition, work well. Recent monitoring indicated that in 2005/06, 45 per cent of managed moves had been successfully taken on roll in their new school, 32 per cent were still on dual placement (partial success) and 25 per cent had returned to the original school – where sometimes the behaviour is improved!

■ Heads reported that dual registration which would operate until the move of a pupil was shown to work was a good thing. Some at least had confidence in that but, 'the Sharing Panels still have to prove themselves'.

■ LSUs have a lot to offer and may work best when they are linked to SEN and EBD work. This was the arrangement in one school, where it was known as the Learning Zone. Renaming it and revaluing it had stopped it being seen as the sin-bin.

■ The findings from interviewing children in one school who had had fixed term exclusions was that they quite liked to be sent home. It was decided to replace three day exclusions by one day exclusions and to use the LSU more.

What is needed

Alternative provision is not a well-developed area. It was said that the facilities available were not known about or used by the schools. College providers of alternative curricula have found it difficult to establish the provision because schools (say they) do not have funding allocated to pay for alternative provision. The uncoordinated nature of it is indicated by one college provider who said, 'I am hoping to sneak in some motor vehicle courses'. The view was that alternative curriculum was a 'dumping ground'. This appears to be another 'revaluing' challenge.

The PRUs, whilst working well, 'are full to bursting and more' and the result is that 'we do not have the capacity to do much outreach ... and no case work with families because of (a shortage of) resources'. Reintegration of Year 9 and 10 pupils is also hampered by a lack of school places. There is a need for more working partnerships between agencies of reasonable size. The establishment and maturing of school clusters would help with issues of this kind, but the difficulties and timescales of these processes should not be underestimated.

The exclusion rate in the central part of the LA has increased due to the exclusion activities of two or three schools and the LA is working on these. There needs to be a range of ways of tackling the issue of the few schools that find it necessary to exclude disproportionate numbers. Not only is there the effect on the children who experience exclusion but it compromises the education community's work on reducing exclusions.

Project follow-up initiative
Background

The team was asked to look at primary school exclusions which had risen during the Autumn term 2007; 35 were permanently excluded in that one term compared with 44 in the whole of 2006/07. Eight primary schools were visited, school statistics were examined and overall permanent and fixed period exclusion figures were scrutinised. LA 1 has over 300 primary schools, 41 clusters and and two EBD special schools. It was widely considered that the legal requirement to organise full time appropriate provision for a pupil excluded for a fixed term period from Day 6 was troubling schools and led to headteachers moving more quickly to permanent exclusion.

What headteachers said about primary school exclusions

The ECM agenda is supposed to address all issues around child care and development; it is still not enough – the systems don't meld.

Social Services are no longer funded to work with the whole family.

Government zero tolerance agenda legitimises for some heads the rejection of children who do not behave well.

The skills are not being thought about. The LA needs to take a fresh look at what it needs to do. There should be more joined up thinking, joined up people.

It's the effective sharing of all the community assets. Some of that thinking needs to be around the cluster/consortia arrangements. Improving communications and holding forums.

Delay in acting is the big issue.

The exclusions budget should be strategically diverted towards prevention. The prevention agenda should be operated more prominently to deal with things before they escalate. The LA needs a permanent group of really good professionals who can pick a child up as a case, provide intervention holistically, sometimes known as practitioner consultants.

Stamina, patience, tolerance and parental engagement are needed by schools and encouragement to go the extra mile. Where parental engagement is seen as a problem, the schools should be supported to persist; lack of parental support should not contribute to the exclusion decision. 'Different heads have different ends of the road'. Some schools have more links, do more bidding for extra money, exploit networks more fully, and have created more options. Heads are aware that there are often 'no boundaries at home'. When does the child learn how to play, how to get on, and 'how to take being corrected and respond adaptively'. However, 'there is so much more you can do with parents at primary phase – more leverage'.

Support of various kinds was called for by primary heads. Where space is available, some schools provide 1:1 contact and time out opportunities. This could be full-time, with some feed into classrooms. Schools wanted counsellors, peer moderators, learning mentoring, playground buddy systems which all help to provide support for the child coming in. Schools needed school and community-based practitioner consultants providing direct support *very quickly* funded by grants for individual children to make permanent exclusion avoidable. Schools still need to find ways to create more internal withdrawal/seclusion areas, and ideally an alternative teaching environment on the site.

Managed moves are a good idea for some children, but it is not a good idea to take a difficult child and put them in an already disruptive or disrupted school. There was an expressed need for more school practitioners, staff mentoring and family support.

Exclusion to get help was a response by headteachers in some cases. Heads often say things like: 'I permanently excluded this time because it's the only way I could see to get help'... and this should become a thing of the past. But then another school is being offered a financial carrot to take the child without any funds being used to address the roots of the problem.

Primary pupil at risk of exclusion cameo

The LA data record the case of a boy who was said to have tried to burn down the school. The fuller background indicates a relatively minor (or less likely to be successful) fire setting incident and myriad background factors which had not been addressed – and many not known about by the school eg. a bereavement. A lesson the LA has taken from this, and which is relevant to other LAs, is that schools sometimes do not spend the time or have the personnel to enquire more deeply. Individual cases sometimes require a case work approach, as much to sort out solutions which will work as to find the causes of difficulty. There is a view that moving towards, and resourcing for, a solution-focused approach has much merit and is a matter both of individual skills and a professional environment that embraces supportive and not punitive strategies.

Discussion at feedback

The feedback to the LA's Behaviour Support Service suggested a range of explanations for raised primary school exclusions:

- Day 6 provision was recognised as a problem by three of the eight schools visited

- PSA money has gone into groups of schools under the consortia budgets and could be perceived by heads as having 'disappeared'. More recently, there has been pupil support funding (£3,000) for managed moves which had not been available previously

- Clusters are not yet committing to not exclude and the LA has to take responsibility for exclusions. Once it is developed and operationalised the Cluster Behaviour Plan will help. Schools do not understand how to play a part in Day 6 and provisional Cluster arrangements have not yet developed to manage this

■ Headteachers' perceptions of permanent exclusions 'not being our problem any more' and thinking that the pupil has gone on to something better or more appropriate. This is accompanied by a diminishing will to go the greater distance and develop a wider range of options

■ Need for more social and family support. Expansion of things already available like voluntary agency and Targeted Family support

■ Local control of money and exercising strategic control is still an uncertain process

■ The permanent exclusion that you do not hear about until it happens

■ The BSS need for schools to work with for a permanently excluded pupil. BSS have a reintegration-readiness scale in use to judge when reintegration will work

■ Linkage to secondary needs consideration – Transition Mentors are working in this area

■ Some heads want external help to solve the problems which they see as beyond them; others use external help to do the job which they still recognise as theirs to do

■ Setting up the one key individual for that pupil is seen as good practice. Good pastoral structures, however informal, could mean that there is always one person the troubled young person can go to, someone who will take a supportive role with the youngster, 'someone special' and not just the Learning Mentor assigned to do a job with 'him'

■ Full information on children is needed and this will help schools have more understanding of the young person's background and of their and other agencies' roles

■ More permanent exclusions mean there is less time for BSS staff to spend in schools.

Forty four exclusions from over 300 primary schools, when it is mostly single exclusions from a school, could be seen as a 'blip', where a small change in regulations has reduced tolerance levels or posed a new problem for which they could see no immediate solution. Day 6 would seem to have contributed to this reaction. It brought to light other needs the primary schools had, and the uncertainties and insecurities evoked by the change to consortia level funding for behaviour. Renewed support and pressure from the support staff and commitment across working clusters should provide the basis for avoiding this unusual rise in future.

Likelihood of success in reducing exclusions

Reducing permanent exclusions by half in LA 1 was thought to be 'quite difficult'. A chart completed by a number of officers and heads provides a picture of needs and an indication of what is working (see Table 4.4).

The table suggests that inclusion units in school are not functioning as the answer and that alternative provision could offer more. But this is currently rated quite low, as is family and community support. By contrast, managed moves and the PRU with reintegration are rated highly, for potential and actual effectiveness. Training of mainstream school staff is seen as needing a higher profile and there are indications that reintegration is not aided by schools unwilling to offer places.

Review of success in reducing exclusions

The rate for permanent exclusion fell in 2007/08. The fall to 0.15 per cent, takes LA 1 out of the top quartile of excluders. If the new network arrangements gel, this could allow the downward trajectory to continue. While the much larger number of secondary exclusions fell by a third, primary permanent exclusions increased by half in the most recent year (though numbers are small). The proportion of total permanent exclusions that are from primary school rose to 20 per cent of LA 1's permanent exclusions, compared with the national average of 14 per cent, which it had been the previous year. This may settle down when cluster arrangements are in place and Day 6 provision is more confidently managed.

LA 1's secondary fixed term exclusions rose from below the national average to approaching 40 per cent above. This is clearly a matter of concern, at the very least in terms of missed schooling and opportunities to learn. Recently, the recording mechanism changed, and though the numbers of exclusions appear to have gone up, electronic registers may just be recording more accurately. There was speculation that they had actually fallen because there was less under-recording. Concern about exclusion rates has been ratched up and this appears to have influenced headteachers. Heightened concern can affect where a headteacher sets the bar but it also encourages officers and others to be more involved in prevention and to be more robust in confronting exclu-

Type of provisions to address exclusions	Use *and* effectiveness of this provisions	How important *could* its role be 5 – 1	How important *is* its role currently 5 – 1
Inclusion units in schools	Some awful, some good – could contribute more especially for children on +6 days FT Ex	4/5, 5	2/4, 1/2
alternative curriculum provision	The more this is developed, the wider the range of choice for pupils...	*4/5, 5*	3/4, 3
Behaviour support (BIP, BEST etc.)	Money has been used effectively		
Integrated multi-agency provision including VCS involvement	No knowledge	*3*	3, 1/2
Focus on family and community support	Parent partnership – supports PEx pupils Support for children with statements. Parent support group	Theory is 5. Practice is not – 4/5.	1 3/4
Managed moves and support for transitions	Yes – we have a support and transition programme for Y6 Timing of managed move has to be right	5	5
PRU with reintegration role	Our service is the frontline for exclusions Hopefully the sharing panels will make it easier to reduce exclusions	5	5
Training of mainstream school staff	The service has fairly good links with staff – TAs come in to observe; Run behaviour management courses. Uptake of courses has reduced over the year. Would like to see more of the pastoral teams in school developing their skills and awareness – are not on top of developments	5	3/4
Special school and out of authority placement	There should be more EBD placements – the children we have with statements we struggle to move on. Authority special schools are full.	5	3
Other	Two pupils in PRU have been ready for M/S for 2/3 months but cannot get them in. It is difficult to get schools to offer places		

Table 4.4: Rating the potential and current importance of various types of service (*5 is very important, 1 is of little or no importance*)

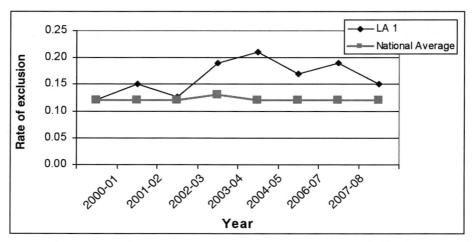

Figure 4.3: Permanent exclusion rates – LA 1 and England 2000-2008

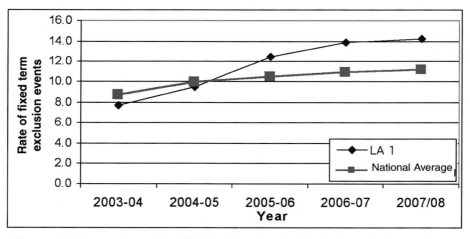

Figure 4.4: Secondary school fixed term exclusion rates – LA 1 and England 2003-2008

sions. More may need to be done at member and senior officer level and greater investment made in the already successful use of managed moves and alternative curriculum provision.

The downward trend in permanent exclusions in the last year is impressive. Consolidation and further progress depends on operating the new local cluster arrangements effectively and increasing the pressure and support from councillors and officers so it is explicit.

With some delegated funding, the school clusters may work to varying degrees but in aggregate still leave LA 1 as a relative high permanent excluder. The clusters need to function to coordinate activities for managed moves and Day 6 provision and the perceived effectiveness of support services needs to be raised. The nature and appropriateness, and therefore the perceived value, of the services may be enhanced by a more exclusive focus on a local patch, but this will need strong drive and not just goodwill. Currently, units in schools, alternative provision and integrated multi-agency provision are seen as less effective than they might be. Similarly, family support is rated as less effective than it actually is and needs to be.

Local authority 2 (LA 2)

Preliminary analysis

The recent history of exclusions in LA 2 shows increasing rates of permanent exclusion until a fall from more than double the national average of 0.12 per cent to 0.18 per cent in 2005/06 when renewed attention was given to the issue of school exclusion. Fixed term exclusions were on a downward trend from a high, which was almost double the national average in 2003/04 and they were slightly above the national average in 2005/06. LA 2's exclusions peaked at Year 9, compared to Year 10 nationally. LA 2 tended to exclude secondary school pupils at a younger age than the national profile.

LA 2 had recently been implementing support services in schools, which reduced permanent exclusions in the previous year by 32 per cent (2005/2006). The focus was on consolidating, highlighting and embedding the current work.

In LA 2, as elsewhere, a tension exists between raising attainment and keeping young people in the classrooms. An inclusive attitude is needed across all schools and agencies. This dilemma is currently being tackled by re-provisioning, having an inclusive attitude and doing deals. It was acknowledged that young people will simply not fit into the school environment in some cases and the need arises to target their behaviour and get them into an environment in which they can remain whilst they learn.

Schools in LA 2 have undergone some changes in personnel over the past three years and this has produced a different outlook. This improvement coincided with the arrival and implementation of BIP, BEST, Healthy Schools and the National Strategy. BIP has been particularly generous in LA 2. This funding has supported Learning Support Unit provision in schools.

Reasons for high rates of exclusion

Stakeholder group attendees discussed the primary causes of exclusions as seen by those working in LA 2. Causes of exclusion were given as:

- Some reasons specific to individual schools, such as leadership issues
- High levels of deprivation: 50 per cent of the population in LA 2 come from the nine worst wards in the country; there is an argument that LA 2's statistical neighbours are not representative of this authority
- Transient population
- 24 per cent of the population are eligible for free school meals. This figure is seen as a serious under-representation because eligible families do not claim free schools meals for fear of being caught for benefit fraud (working in addition to claiming assistance). The figure should more realistically be 50 per cent. The government allocation per pupil received by the LA is lower than it should be because parents are not disclosing their true financial status
- Young people and their families have particularly low aspirations – for example, a bright girl with high attainment wanting to be a beautician
- There is a problem with young people taking time off school to earn money during seasonal periods with the consequence that attendance levels are variable depending on the time of year.

Assets available

The council had registered its commitment to bring down exclusions and appointed a new Head of EBSD and EOTAS. She engaged in a year-long series of discussions with schools and agencies through the Behaviour Strategy Group to set in place arrangements, a workforce and initiatives to better manage LA 2's excessive exclusions. The assets are as set out below.

1. The Learning Support Unit provides support for 1 to 3 days, with the following rationale:

- the pupil must deal with the problem
- there are logical consequences for behaviour
- it is formal and serious
- but then becomes somewhere for pupils to begin to develop relationships
- they follow a timetable to structure life in the unit.

The LSU provides 'a short, sharp shock for pupils who did something silly and made a mistake – they don't come back'. The 'more disturbed' ones who do come back are treated with different approaches.

2. Managed transfers to another mainstream school. 'A fresh start is often sufficient to see the pupil move on positively, to give them another try.'

3. The Inclusion Support Team is made up of members from several disciplines: CAMHS, school nurse, family-school liaison officer, EP and behaviour advisory teacher. Each school is allocated its own IST worker who will lead on a multi-agency approach to support pupils. They can refer children and their families to interventions. The IST remit is to manage all excluded pupils coming from the schools or going back into school. They are still a new service and at the time of the interviews there were indications that they had yet to be firmly embedded into the existing structure. Also available in schools are teaching support assistants and learning mentors. A reintegration officer is optional for schools. A Pupils Welfare Officer is also available to schools and is well used.

4. A good deal of resources have gone into addressing and unpicking the problems of attendance.

5. Aimhigher is operating in LA 2 and this generally raises the aspirations of young people (Teachernet, 2008).

6. Barnardos have been focusing on offering parenting classes as a way of addressing the poor aspirations of young people and their families.

7. LA 2 has been allocated funding from the Respect Agenda for parenting support services.

8. A link has been established with a neighbouring low excluding LA which has a range of creative alternative provisions and managed moves etc.

9. LA 2 discusses ways of reintegrating young people into school. This is done by assessing the child and deciding whether being back in the school is best for the child. They try to be as flexible as possible.

10. Work is underway towards personalised learning plans which should ultimately eliminate exclusions completely.

11. Young people could be placed with the PRU without being excluded from school.

The secondary school inclusion cameo below indicates the growing strengths of one school in LA 2 and its potential as a model of inclusion practice.

Secondary school inclusion cameo

School B had eight permanent exclusions in each of the previous two school years and none in the most recent. LA officers stated that until recently 'schools were not on board but are now'. From an uncoordinated and indivi-dualist position, the heads were reported as now 'responding really well in finding creative solutions'. School B's headteacher stated his reasons for not permanently excluding were that now he no longer needed to because of the systems and initiatives they had set in place in the school and he could tele-phone the Head of Behaviour Services if close to exclusion and ask if there were 'any facilities available at your end'. The school had been funded to set up an EDB support teacher, a learning support teacher, pastoral managers (non-teacher qualified) and a behaviour manager. They had established a nurture group, a seclusion unit and extended the learning support unit. The school had learning mentors who have the necessary time to counsel pupils and, with the pastoral managers, make supportive contact with the home.

The head described the school as the most challenged in the authority, with large numbers of transient pupils. He was not under pressure with regard to attainment, though teaching had improved and results were better. He did not feel under pressure from the LA not to exclude. 'It is not that pupils are behav-ing differently, just that less is getting onto my desk'.

Touring the school, it was obvious that the inclusion facilities were well-staffed, in good accommodation and worked with a healthy buzz.

The year-long Behaviour Strategy Group review had been important and this had led to the regulated High Needs Admissions System which meant that even the school which was fully subscribed took a share of the non standard admissions. The multi-agency Integrated Support Team (IST) has been vital because before 'things had not been joined up'; IST is 'a very hands-on group of workers'. The in-school support team is strong and necessary because 'even with the IST workers, you have to wait'.

The combination of LA-wide negotiated provision, new systems and greater workforce diversification within the school enabled a level of inclusion not con-sidered possible before, but was something the school was now extremely proud of.

What is working

Though there is not a sense of the job completed, there is considerable satisfaction at the impact of the new arrangements which are contributing to bringing exclusions down and providing better for excluded children. The task of addressing values and principles has clearly been done and may have been the achievement of the Behaviour Strategy Group. 'The ECM agenda is our agenda'. Much more than elsewhere, a recognition is expressed of the needs and rights of at risk young people.

- The High Needs Admissions System (HNAS) is transparent, broadly conceived and appears to have widespread sign-up. This may continue to cater for the transient, excluded and hard to place young people as well as for In-Year Fair Admissions. The HNAS needs careful monitoring. It still rests largely on 'good relationships' and peer pressure and was acknowledged as vulnerable.

- Interviews with senior LA staff, Springboard, Behaviour and Attendance Consultant, a voluntary provider, Police, councillor and union representatives signalled how much was going on and how far the Authority had travelled.

- Child and Adolescent Therapeutic Services, Barnardos (parenting support), Active-8 (volunteer mentoring) and Homestart (parenting support, leisure and outreach) contribute also. As one LA officer said, 'We commission all over the place. There is a quite fertile voluntary sector out there'. Nonetheless, some providers consider that they have greater capacity and are not sufficiently used.

- The reorganisation to three area bases for services must have merit and one awaits its impact. Springboard (NRF-funded) was clearly the sort of initiative welcomed in terms of its focus on 'the really hard end' and its way of operating to offer all-round support. This is all still new and its interface with schools will need to be carefully negotiated to promote inclusion and reintegration.

- The multi-site PRU is a valuable resource for receiving youngsters, assessing and providing clear, trusted accounts of problems and likely success of reintegration. Some good results have been achieved.

- Managed transfers have a part to play. An actual enforced move is not in every case a bad thing but managed transfer can achieve a better outcome, even if the transfer is to the PRU.

- Schools' responses to exclusions show a commitment to finding alternatives. Clearly they work hard to activate an inclusion policy. Comments from a range of interviewees included the following:

With primary schools, heads are keen to hold on to children, support and not exclude them.

They seek advice on children without mentioning the names of children who are at risk of being excluded.

The heads have responded really well in finding creative solutions.

The rationale here is early intervention and prevention.

- Alternative curriculum and Increased Freedom of the Curriculum (IFC) give clear possibilities. Alternative curricula are intended to increase pupil engagement by offering more appropriate courses. College type expertise provides links with industry and commerce.

  In a perfect world, every child has an IEP and if it is appropriate they can access college-style courses, content and relationships all properly resourced.

  Community-based activities are available too.

- A central LA agent to collate and coordinate in this area would be helpful. The child out of school placed in an alternative menu can keep him/her in education – however broadly conceived. It would be important to monitor if behaviour referrals at KS 4 reduce as a consequence of a more YP-friendly diet.

- Fixed term exclusion have a limited role to play and schools' ownership of their own children and the layering of provision that can be made for them keep fixed term exclusions lower.

- The tremendous reduction in permanent exclusion has to be recognised and celebrated at every level. *It used to be 40 – 50 excluded; now it is 40-50 out of school but they are receiving alternative provision.*

What is needed

The possibilities in LA 2 for alternative provision and work experience are very limited and need further investigation and development. Developing a personalised curriculum for individual pupils within the schools is very difficult; this is possible in the PRU. The PRU centres are highly regarded by the pupils and parents. Whilst the high quality of provision should be maintained, the balance of effort should turn to more reintegration and better reintegration packages. Alternative provision is vital. The FE College as a partner in developing provision for the right young people, could, with appropriate funding, extend its offer.

Collaboration with the College is good and, across the community, there was recognition that things needed to change: '*We could do with more roll-on roll-off courses; more flexibility is needed. More opportunities*'.

Alternative Curriculum opportunities are being devised in school also at KS 4. It was also suggested it would be good to get more engagement from local businesses to provide alternative curriculum.

There are issues with the funding of PRUs; schools do not contribute fully to funding the PRU and the one PRU in LA 2 (across several sites) has four times the rate of pupils in PRU provision than the national average. It is difficult for schools to contribute more as budgets are currently in deficit.

Integrated Children's Services consists of the Education Service and Social Services for children and can accommodate voluntary agency contributions. Some services were considered vital – but slow to respond and having '*impossible waiting lists*', while others '*could be used much more effectively*'.

Pupils' and parents' voices may not be heard to the degree they need to be. More listening to the needs, views and complaints of young people. It helps if there is someone they can go and talk to to defuse situations.

Alternative management of the one-off incident normally deemed to warrant a permanent exclusion should be considered.

Change of attitude was thought to be needed – or *further* change of attitude. '*Don't ask 'is this behaviour acceptable or unacceptable?' ask what it means*'. The example given was of a mother of a 'difficult' boy. She had cystic fibrosis which was a big problem at home. Her son was worried that she might die. Once the school learned about this, it became more understanding of his behaviour.

Project follow-up initiative
The third phase was to be an *action* phase, working with LA 2 and its schools; in reality such intervention is difficult. What has been found useful is engaging in further enquiry and contributing to discussions about alternative approaches or how to sustain and spread promising work already underway. Three tasks were agreed: an examination of provision for excluded pupils through visits to and observations in PRUs; gathering evidence on the perspective of primary schools; getting the views of front-line teachers in one secondary school.

Visiting two PRU centres to interview children provided a picture of spacious accommodation and well structured programmes. Attainment or attendance data or reintegration rates were not investigated, but conversations suggest that the last of these is not high and the High Needs Admissions Protocol may not be working effectively in this area. The number of 300 being educated out of school was mentioned and has to be considered high for a small LA. It is obvious that the role of the PRU provision has moved from what some saw as a youth-oriented (youth club?) provision to serious educational placements. However, the numbers placed there are a concern, as are the limited prospects for adjusting its role and extending preventative and reintegration work alongside other professionals eg. Behaviour and Attendance Leaders in schools.

Reintegration and managed moves, whether from school to school or via PRUs, remain a challenge. But it must be remembered that a lot of the funding beyond the AWPU is 'deprivation' funding. When all funding is included, the spend per pupil shows that in LA 2 there is a range across the eight secondary schools of £1,400, with the largest being 36 per cent higher than the lowest (or least deprived). The differential might need reconsideration (and making greater) and the moneys moving with the challenging young person might be greater – or even money to ensure retention. Greater delegation to school clusters in the three areas might have merit if tied to an assured responsibility for continued education of at risk children. The message was that pupils at risk of exclusion need appropriate and sustained support. 'Lift them out of the environment, do something different with them, offer them new opportunities, have somewhere that would accept them the way they are when they are ready to try and reintegrate. Don't give up on them – be persistent'.

Primary headteachers interviewed in a group reported certain issues relating to support for behaviour. The heads were frustrated at the amount of paperwork involved and the delays this entailed, and wanted quick and practical support for pupils at risk of exclusion. Most of the frustration of headteachers stemmed from their wish to send children home for half a day or a whole day, after an incident or upset, without making it a fixed term exclusion. At the same time, they want such action brokered by the LA and family link work to be done by Behaviour Support. Their approach has been to use this as a way of working in *partnership* with the parents. There is tension between this working in partnership with parents, as the headteachers see it, and what the law requires. This is an area where frank, conciliatory discussions are needed to develop an acceptable way forward.

Enhanced Resource Facilities or Learning Support Unit (LSU) provision was valued. However, frustration was expressed at being made to wait when places were known to be available in units, though travel problems sometimes made it difficult. They acknowledged that the two term placements at a unit worked for some but that others had been there for four days a week over a longer period.

Six staff of one secondary school interviewed noted that exclusions had decreased markedly in recent years and said they focused on 'retention'. They asserted that 'staff must have inclusive attitudes'. They reeled off a range of initiatives within the school – LSU, Inclusion, Mind, creative learning pathways – designed to provide for those who struggle with behaviour. 'If we permanently exclude, we've failed'. Undoubtedly headteachers are responding well to the inclusion/ECM agenda and finding creative solutions.

They noted also the challenges, such as doing 100+ non-routine admissions in a year. Fifty per cent of the NRAs are reportedly poor attenders and 'You never get anything extra with a high needs admission'. They lamented that mental health difficulties were not addressed and that there were long waiting times for CAMHS. The school, however, uses a range of services.

The police and PSCOs reported important support and presence from officers in schools and good team work. Some exclusions puzzled them (eg. for drugs) as the exclusions put young people further at risk and do not address the root problem – which they are equipped to provide for. There was admiration for the work of inclusion units, which had 'kept 2,000 kid-days off the street'. While more can be done on the preventive front, in terms of better provision and diversionary activity for young people, a lot is clearly going on.

Likelihood of success in reducing exclusions by half

This question put to interviewees provoked mixed responses ranging from a tentative, 'Yes, it is possible', through to 'We are already on the way'. There was even a resounding 'Yes, we could go to nil exclusions. I am very optimistic about getting down to zero'.

It is notable that the scoring in Table 4.5 (overleaf) shows relatively high levels of importance given to current working of most elements of provision and smaller differences between the actual and the ideal than with many LAs. Training of mainstream school staff is where the biggest difference lies. Managed moves also are not currently felt to be working or workable in the way that might be expected.

Type of provisions to address exclusions	Use *and* effectiveness of this provisions	How important *could* its role be	How important *is* its role currently
Inclusion units in schools		5, 5, 4, 5	5, 4, 3
Alternative curriculum provision		*4, 5, 5*	*3, 3*
Behaviour support (BIP, BEST etc.)		5, 5, 3/4	3/4, 5
Integrated multi-agency provision including VCS involvement	*List other agencies involved. List VCS involvement and its scale*	*5, 4*	*3, 4*
Focus on family and community support		5, 5, 5	5, 3
Managed moves		5, 5, 5	3, 2/3, 4
PRU with reintegration role		5, 3, 5	5, 1, 4
Training of mainstream school staff		5, 5	3, 2
Special school and out of authority placement		3	1

Table 4.5: Rating the potential and current importance of various types of service (*5 is very important, 1 is of little or no importance*)

Review of progress in reducing exclusions

The reduction of permanent exclusions from 40 to 17 and then 7 in 2007/08 is a tremendous achievement. It is evident that this is because of initiatives set in place, within and outside schools, following the Behaviour Strategy Group meetings. Reductions in permanent exclusions appear to be a consequence of structural arrangements in the secondary schools (special centres, personalised learning), new roles (Learning Mentors, Pastoral Managers), faith that key support is available outside the school and a senior officer available for advice, problem solving and solutions. There remains, however, a problem of exclusions for one-off incidents. Of Behaviour Managers, it was said, 'I do not know what we would do without them'. Of relations with the LA, 'You felt you were on the same page', and there was much appreciation for the LA support. As one secondary headteacher said, 'No one from the LA has put me under pressure not to exclude'. In the current year he had found it unnecessary to do so.

Fixed term exclusions (instances) went up by a quarter in 2006/07, seeming to compensate for the decrease in permanents. The rate continued upwards to almost twice the national average in 2007/08. It is almost certain that there are fewer days of education lost than would be the case if permanent exclusions had remained high. Day 6 requirements, once understood by schools, may reduce lost education further.

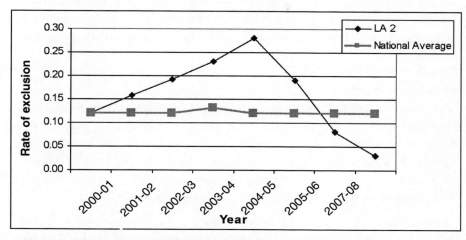

Figure 4.5: Permanent exclusion rates – LA 2 and England

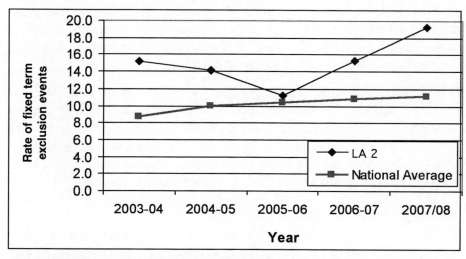

Figure 4.6: Secondary school fixed term exclusion rates – LA 2 and England

An LA officer said, 'Schools manage 95 per cent of their children magnificently. The inclusion agenda does not mean that we can include *all* pupils in schools in the way they are set up and operate currently'.

The optimistic commitment was voiced that one should 'influence thinking through practice; do it differently and hope everyone else catches you up, hopefully'. That does not do justice to the strategically driven political and professional will to bring down permanent exclusions. Discussion with school headteachers in the Behaviour Review Group led to agreed plans and funding and implementation has been a dynamic, robust continuing of that engagement, with great appreciation shown for the efforts of all partners.

Local authority 3 (LA 3)
Preliminary analysis
LA 3 has six secondary schools, 36 primary schools, a special school and a Pupil Referral Unit. Permanent exclusions in the secondary schools fell from a high of 40 in 2004/05 to 24 in the following year. At the same time there was a fairly constant number of fixed term exclusions from 2003/04 to 2005/06 – 600 to 611 to 601. With the work of the Learning Support Centres developing, there were prospects of reducing both sets of figures..

Despite some claims, there are few indications of greater difficulties encountered with LA 3 children in terms of deprivation, unemployment and transience. LA 3 has been above the national average since 1999 but the rates of permanent exclusion became very much worse 2003/04 and 2004/05; to be at the national average, exclusion numbers would need to be 18 (0.12%). Different schools clearly have different needs and challenges and, as elsewhere, permanent exclusions are not spread evenly across the authority's schools.

It is notable that, in this high excluding area, census data from 2001 and indices of deprivation from 2004 indicate that, compared with the national average, LA 3 has less deprivation, fewer lone parent households, fewer adults with no qualifications and lower crime rates. Achievement at key stages 1, 2 and 3 is also above average yet the rates of permanent exclusion have been half as high again as the nearest LA within the statistical neighbours group.

Reasons for high exclusions
The three town schools have similar problems. One had previously been in special measures and the perception was that it had more than its share of disadvantaged pupils, receiving a high number of excluded pupils, pupils with SEN etc. It was, until recently, always undersubscribed. Another was usually full and fully subscribed, with a new head who had been deputy at another town secondary. The third town secondary school was a source of concern a few years ago but is now oversubscribed. The retiring head at the start of the project was a big excluder, accounting for half of all exclusions in the authority, yet he reduced the number of permanent exclusions to near zero in his last year, when his LSC opened.

The two out of town schools are very popular and exclude few pupils: one has become significantly more ethnically diverse in recent years. The only voluntary aided school in area is the highest GCSE 5 A-C rates, is always full and, while it does not tend to exclude, neither does it often take excluded pupils.

The stakeholder group comprised senior offices, Youth Offending Service, Connexions, the PRU and one secondary headteacher. Later meetings actually became a secondary heads forum, timed to occur when they had their meetings together with the LA. Discussing the current rate of permanent and fixed term exclusions in LA 3, they stated that they were confident that the reported figures reflected the true picture and that informal exclusions were not occurring. It was felt that some children would benefit from supported transitions and very early intervention to prevent difficulties escalating to the point where the children could no longer be worked with. There was general agreement that the PRU has been a victim of its own success in that some children actively want to go there.

Causes	Responses
Persistent low level disruption and non-compliance from pupils	Programme of staff development Important to retain staff to ensure stability for children
Strong position taken by heads on disruptive behaviour	This has led to high exclusions but good PRU provision PRU has good outcomes but many pupils still enter NEET on leaving at 16
Pupil anger management issues, lack of social skills and coping mechanisms	Use of reflection sheets and learner support units
Lack of early intervention and identification of learning difficulties	Developing better multi-agency working
Inconsistency of staff responses to behaviour	
Tradition of exclusions in LA 3	
Three schools in the town centre are quite clustered together and have a similar profile/demographic; managed moves may, therefore, need to be outside of these three	Learning Support Centres opened in three school
School choice and subsequent travel to school	
No managed move protocol	
Perception of the value and efficacy of education by some pupils – linked to low aspiration	Work on relationship between school and parent Need for alternative curriculum

Table 4.6: Perceived causes of exclusion and reported responses

Table 4.6 summarises some of the perceived causes of exclusion and the identified responses. Learning support units were recently established in three of the schools and a fourth is planning one. Staff training has taken place and continues.

Assets available

This small LA has a number of assets, some of which may be under-exploited or not fully developed. For the most part the assets lie within schools and the strengths to be found there may need to be valued more and applied with greater confidence.

1. Attendance is not a significant issue – it is generally quite good. Have a mostly effective EWS

2. There is some cross-border movement. However, the majority of the LA's cohort are educated in LA 3 and cross border exclusions are not an issue (recently excluded a cross border student and kept him in their own PRU as opposed to sending back to own LA, as it was thought to be best for the student, who was in Yr 11).

3. There is good provision for LAC – get good additional support in school.

4. There has been a significant decrease in LA 3's teen pregnancy rate – attributed partly to the placement of school based drop-ins in three schools.

5. A good counselling service operated by a voluntary body.

6. An EBD special school in a nearby LA which 'manages' and LA 3 just 'contributes pupils'. Currently, 10-12 pupils are placed there at a cost of £17,000 per year each.

7. LA 3 does not have VCS providers for the secondary sector as the authority does not meet any disadvantage criteria. There is NCH and MIND involvement in primary schools but for secondary alternative curriculum provision, the only VCS is a project for motor vehicle skills, part funded by LSC.

8. No protocol for managed moves – no formal agreement between Heads but moves do occur particularly for looked after children (LAC).

9. They have an Increased Flexibility Programme – schools are allocated places at the local college but there is little provision at the college for young people with SEN or who disaffected. The college does not provide a broad range of vocational options – young people need to go to a neighbouring borough for this.

10. The town schools have just opened LSCs and use these as internal exclusion units and to provide support. Another is on the way.

11. The PRU has 30 full time places but is currently not at capacity. It was last inspected in Summer 2005. Due to a recent decrease in permanent exclusions it started to provide support in schools to prevent exclusions – this has so far been limited but an outreach service is developing. The PRU supports reintegration into education but is not used for fixed term exclusions and there is no requirement to have EP involvement before entry. They try to retain the older pupils for the Year 10-11 curriculum and deal with Years 7-9 in school. The PRU also has a small number of school refusers in it. The costs is about £12,000 per annum per pupil.

What is working

The LA has helped schools improve their in-school provision for challenging pupils and views the primary school scene as unproblematic.

- The LA has developed a good pathway approach in the case of support in primary schools for exclusion using a multi-agency approach. This is being extended to secondary schools
- Some LA 3 secondary schools are operating Consistent Management and Cooperative Discipline (CMCD is an American programme developed by Jerry Freiberg) with reported success
- The use of one school's LSC was discussed and the policy of celebrating success, for example, through graduations every six weeks applauded (Though the head noted that about one in six of the 'graduates' experienced further problems)
- Three new LSCs have been introduced – two within the last year. These could have an impact on the profile of exclusions; one result was that there were more exclusions of Year 11 pupils and fewer lower down the school and this is being monitored
- Primary school permanent exclusions are not an issue in LA 3 – a discussion was held around whether it would be possible to move to nil exclusions. One reason for low exclusions was thought to be the closeness of relationship between primary schools and parents.

What is needed

Staff training is an ongoing need. Frontline staff need to have a better understanding of pupil needs and experience greater partnership working between support provided outside the classroom and that given inside.

In discussing a managed move protocol, whereby headteachers would be obliged to take pupils if their school represented the best environment, it was agreed that headteachers would be against a policy of being forced to accept pupils on managed moves unless all headteachers signed up to it. LA 3 schools are nearing, if not over, capacity and protocols have previously been necessary to protect those schools which have had capacity from receiving a disproportionate number of managed moves. Discussions should achieve agreement among all six headteachers.

Difficulties are being experienced around reintegration. Managed moves were thought to help young people start afresh. This is complicated by the fact that three high excluding schools are geographically close together so a fresh start away from previous peer groups, relations etc may be harder to achieve and a solution to this is needed.

A question was raised: what do you do when a child is excluded from school due to violence to staff? Managed moves are seen to be out of the question but the PRU still accepts and deals with this behaviour. Currently, more girls are experiencing difficulties in school than previously and the PRU has seen a rise in female admissions. This needs attention and possibly requires some gender-specific input.

Although EPs still have to fulfil their statutory responsibilities, schools can use them how they wish. The claim is that they are currently short of EP time in LA 3 schools; it was thought EPs would do more preventative work if they had more time. Currently, EPs are not used as much as would be helpful for dealing with problem behaviour. Most permanently excluded pupils have only seen the EP once.

Finance is an issue and there is no BIP funding for secondary provision in LA 3, although an officer suggested that schools seem to have more money now for behavioural support.

Certain outside agencies, projects and initiatives are under-used. Some might take time to enlarge to scale eg. Youth Line; Education Business Partnership; Oakwood Youth Challenge; Wilderness Expertise; Prince's Trust. Other agencies also have offers – eg. YOT, Connexions – for interventions which could be booked, and could be scaled up if it is what schools want or need. The Integrated Pathways, Pupil Referral Service, Family and Adolescent Support Team all have merit and can work effectively together, and convincingly meet the needs which headteachers identify. The relationship between the LA and schools was questioned and consideration may need to be given to the influence of the LA in practice and how this might be beefed up.

More opportunities are needed for alternative curriculum. The FE College involvement, a partner in developing provision for, as they sometimes express it 'the right young people', would help though they have recently changed from a rolling programme to fixed entrance points. Increased Freedom of the Curriculum (IFC) gives clear possibilities. A central agent to collate and coordinate in this area would be helpful. Children out of school who are provided with an alternative learning menu can be kept in education – however broadly that is conceived.

An increase in pastoral roles in school is called for – learning mentors, pastoral managers, family workers. Properly accommodated, well-integrated within a school's workforce, such a broadening of the school's workforce can address a wider set of issues in the lives of young people and families.

Project follow-up initiative

Following an initial stakeholder meeting, a period of data gathering, and analysis and feedback to a headteacher group, two further steps were proposed: a review of the inclusion units set up in three schools, and an audit of children at risk of permanent exclusion in the six secondary schools. In addition, a review of the last year's exclusion statistics was carried out and the budget allocations to schools were examined with particular attention to 'deprivation' funding.

Learning Support Centres

Two members of the project team visited LSCs in three secondary schools. The objective was to see how these were structured and the extent to which they do and could function as preventative facilities to avoid exclusion, help to develop pro-school behaviours and maintain the young people's education.

The centres specifically for those at risk of exclusion differed notably across the three schools (and presumably in the school due to open a centre the following summer). It is good that the staff from these centres have met to compare, discuss and plan. It was evident that there was rich experience and high calibre expertise spread across the centres.

Two of the schools offer a three week programme for KS 3 pupils and one school offers a six week programme. The length of the programme is not necessarily the crucial element, though it is important that the return to the mainstream classroom is not made more difficult. There is assessment, a very structured programme and wide liaison. The best features of the programmes are:

- The referral systems where heads of year receive and collate information on candidates for the centre
- Observation before they come to the centre so that some diagnosis can be made of the presenting problems
- Close communication with the families and a 'signing up' to the programme by parents and the young person
- Follow-up back into the classroom by a learning mentor and a continuing thread of support
- Referrals to other agencies, statutory and voluntary, which can contribute to meeting the needs of these young people
- Involvement of mainstream classroom teachers who know what is going on with pupils referred by them and who take advice from centre staff about behaviour management when the child returns ie. the child is not sent away to be 'fixed' and then returns.

It is evident that these units engage in a *behaviour 4 learning* approach where the goal is to support the young person to continue their education and not drop out or be excluded. Special needs expertise is essential for some staff working in the units; some children are judged to be overlooked or experience delays in autistic spectrum diagnosis.

Such centres, or related special needs units, can serve as respite for particular lessons for the young person (or the teacher), can respond to flare-ups and incidental problems which arise and fulfil an induction function for those returning from fixed term exclusion, from the PRU or those arriving on managed moves. There are considerable advantages to having a structured arrangement for a set period of time for a designated client group. Where it can be allied to flexibility that also has merits where it does not disturb a well-functioning preventative facility. It is useful to see measures before the children come in, when they leave and some while later to monitor impact and its durability (eg. AMD). The quality of the accommodation needs to be high, the staffing sound and valued and the sense of being an integral part of the school's provision strong. In the preventative mode, the opportunity to bring in Year 6s who will join the school in September has great promise. The whole needs strong coordination meshing with KS 4 provision, restorative justice, peer mentoring, use of time-out cards and the application of other initiatives (eg. small group behaviour change programme; close monitoring programme).

These are promising developments likely to become standard provision in every school taking its Every Child Matters responsibilities seriously. Schools with the greatest challenges will need to design and fund their provision to meet recognised needs and take preventative action. The Learning Support Centres appear to be functioning well as part of that effort.

At risk of exclusion audit

The numbers identified as at risk of exclusion naturally vary by school. It is clear that, while managed moves might play a part, there is merit in keeping the problem you know in your own school rather than passing it on. Managed moves properly and carefully brokered can support the individual and the system where a breakdown in relationships has taken place. School collectivities can work to support headteachers in their inclusion efforts. The likelihood of this is enhanced where clear systems operate, well supported by the LA.

School	At risk of permanent exclusion numbers
School a	26
School b	8
School c	24
School d	7
School e	0
School f	7
Total	**72**

Table 4.7: Total at risk students by secondary school in LA 3

	Boys	Girls	Totals
Year 7	1	0	1
Year 8	7	0	7
Year 9	21	4	25
Year 10	19	5	24
Year 11	10	5	15
Totals	**58**	**14**	**72**

Table 4.8: At risk of permanent exclusion by sex and year in LA 3 secondary schools

Year 9 appears to be a troubling year, especially for boys. Preventative initiatives (Inclusion Unit programmes etc.) appear to be greatly needed. Nearly 60 per cent of those identified were school action plus or statemented. Fifty per cent of the boys in the group at risk of exclusion were at KS 4 while for the girls it was 71 per cent. Specific strategies aimed at these older girls are needed.

These are amongst the biggest challenges a school faces. Two strategic points emerge: firstly, it is likely that over one third of those who do end up excluded will not be on this list – they will be the one-off incident, so arrangements other than exclusion will probably work better; secondly, 72 pupils is a manageable number viewed across an authority. These young people can be monitored and nurtured, contained and restored to the mainstream if the disproportionate attention needed is given to them – and their families.

Likelihood of success in reducing permanent exclusions by half
'Possible (2006/07); likely (2007/08)'.

'*50:50*'.

'*If secondary outreach was properly funded and was successful in supporting staff and children. If there was a focus on outreach and supporting families. There is a big chance of improving in LA 3 but capacity is an issue*'.

Not a lot of incentive. Might work if threatened with money cuts – or given money to not exclude. Schools care about money and high achievement.

Based on current situation and circumstances, not good; we reduced last year but it is going the other way now.

Type of provisions to address exclusions	Use *and* effectiveness of this provisions	How important *could* its role be	How important *is* its role currently
Inclusion units in schools		5, 4, 5	2, 3
Alternative curriculum provision		*5, 4, 5*	*2, 1*
Behaviour support (BIP, BEST etc.)		5, 5, 5	2, 2
Integrated multi-agency provision including VCS involvement	*List other agencies involved. List VCS involvement and its scale*	5, 5, 5	*3, 2*
Focus on family and community support		*5, 5, 5*	1, 2
Managed moves		5, 3/4	0, 1
PRU with reintegration role		5, 5	3, 3
Training of mainstream school staff		5, 5	1, 3
Special school and out of authority placement			

Table 4.9: Rating the potential and current importance of various types of service (5 is very important, 1 is of little or no importance)

Table 4.9 indicates that there are large differences in the rating of what is available and how important and effective it could be. This points to improvements across the board on alternative curriculum, multi-agency teams; family and community focus, managed moves and staff training. These are not without cost implications.

Review of success

Permanent exclusions in LA 3 schools have fallen from a high of 40 in 2004/05 to 29 then 26 before a rise to 29 again in 2007/08. The explanation for the rise in the most recent year was given as large numbers from one school. At the same time, fixed term exclusions were at or slightly below the national average, with a substantial drop in 2007/08. With the work of the Learning Support Centres developing, one can see the prospect of both sets of figures reducing.

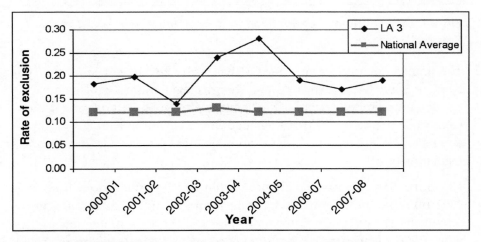

Figure 4.7: Permanent exclusion rates – LA 3 and England

Small numbers, a supportive relationship between LA officers and the six secondary schools and an effective PRU mean that good provision is made for pupils at risk of exclusion and for those permanently excluded. With PRU outreach, general support (and pressure) for the schools with high exclusions, new commitment to inclusion and commendation for low exclusion should bring permanent exclusions to the same downward trajectory as the creditable trend in fixed term exclusions.

There is a shared concern about levels of exclusion and a guarded interest from schools in reducing them. One school would opt for no (permanent) exclusions. While cooperation across the six secondary schools is not strong in this area, greater unity of purpose is developing and should not be difficult to achieve.

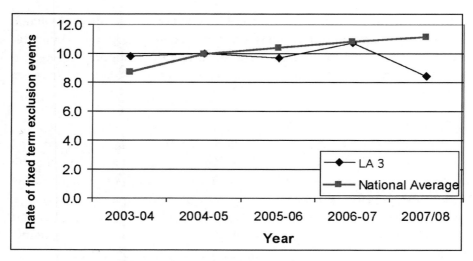

Figure 4.8: Secondary school fixed term exclusion rates – LA3 and England

The ambiguous position of the PRU has many advantages but better coherence would be achieved by establishing a greater outreach role, more contracted, time-limited receipt of challenging young people, and reintegration support. The situation has to be avoided where the PRU is a dumping ground and its role is 'firefighting'. The LA could be more proactive in ensuring and regulating this.

Like other LAs, LA3 worried about not fulfilling legal obligations from Sept 2007 (full-time replacement education from day 6). If children are out of school, the expectation is that school clusters will have the money and *the responsibility*. It is recognised that schools vary in practice, severity and tolerance. Some schools reduced exclusions greatly. There is a view that 'keeping them in' may be better than 'passing them around'. LSCs in three schools have contributed greatly to this development and ways need to be found to increase incentives for schools to look after their own and provide the support where exclusions threaten to rise. Well managed transfer can help – but only if the PRU role is strong, and can act as a layer of provision, as an intermediary and if it can carry out assessments.

Increasing the amount and the integration of inter-agency working, offering more alternative curriculum and encouraging a more diversified workforce in schools all contribute to lower rates of exclusion and better chances for the pupils who drop out or who are dropped out. 'Funding, funding, funding' may be the cry from schools, yet through budget devolution, schools have more of the money than ever before. Headteachers are the ones who can to make key financial decisions and they might usefully consider what they would commission collectively from funds which they control.

Local authority 4

Preliminary analysis

LA 4 had been amongst the highest permanent excluders in the country, often occupying the position of leading permanent excluder. There were falls and rises in the rate of permanent exclusion up to 2005/06, though it remained at more than 50 per cent above the national average. For almost every year from 2001 to 2006, the permanent exclusion rate from secondary schools was more than double the national average rate. In 2006/07, seven secondary schools excluded at double the national rate. Forty two of the 96 secondary school exclusions come from three schools.

LA 4 records fixed term exclusions at a lower level than the national average. The claim is made that the exclusions recorded for LA 4 are accurate and that this partly accounts for high figures; other informants indicate that LA 4 is little different from other LAs where there are examples of informal exclusion, however subtly contrived.

LA 4 was early and enthusiastic in devolving funding to schools. There is a history of many secondary schools in LA 4 taking up grant maintained status in the early 1990s. The secondary schools have preserved an unusual degree of autonomy; academies within the authority's boundaries operate with little or no communication with the authority. This has led to very slimmed down central services and diminished influence and authority in schools, 'The schools are largely autonomous in the way they operate'. LA 4 is one of the most devolved authorities in the country, leaving few resources at its centre.

In terms of provision for permanent exclusion, LA 4 has six PRUs which are usually full at the start of the academic year because reintegration has proved difficult. Some consideration was being given to opening a further PRU! The separation of LA 4 and its schools was evident from the management of the Behaviour Improvement Project (BIP) money. This was managed by the Excellence in Cities (EiC) cluster and the annual reports to the DfES were not seen by the LA.

The LA claims that high priority is given to reducing exclusions, but 'without support, without doing anything', as one headteacher saw it. LA 4 was willing to call in help from outside and regional advisors of various sorts played a part in strategy discussion groups – even if these, and the various research projects over the years, have scarcely affected the exclusion rates.

The LA provides a good deal of glossy documentation of good content. But arguably, this was not matched by robust officer engagement with schools. One officer referred to the tension between secondary schools and the authority as 'hugely stressful and very time-consuming'. Without sustained, supportive and challenging interaction with schools, a shared ethos does not develop and the view taken in some schools and amongst some professionals was that the problem was located in the children, not with the schools and services that are collectively funded and given the remit to educate all learners including challenging young people.

Reasons for high rates of exclusion

A discussion was held with stakeholders in LA 4 to determine the primary causes of school exclusion and the current responses. At risk children are concentrated in a few schools and the situation is exacerbated by the many independent schools which cream off top pupils. Neighbouring boroughs export many children, but with the arrival of new academies and technology colleges this is now changing. It is said that BIP money takes a while to manifest itself, and that systems are slow to develop and implement and the effect on behaviour is a long term outcome.

Permanent exclusions are concentrated in a small number of secondary schools and Figure 4.2 (p35) indicates that LA 4 secondary schools have had extraordinarily high rates of permanent exclusion for a long period.

A PRU place costs the LA £14,000-£18,000 per head, with the school bearing £10,000 of that cost. There are 48 primary places in the PRU, which is always full. Children have to go through the EP and then onto a waiting list. There is the roll out of SEAL across LA 4 to tackle behaviour issues holistically as it is seen as 'embedded behaviour'.

Table 4.9 indicates the sorts of causes identified by the stakeholder group and the reported responses.

A range of views was expressed in the interviews about the high permanent exclusion rates. It was suggested that officially the reduction in permanent exclusion is given higher priority but that officials and headteachers are perhaps too willing to acknowledge that there are occasions where there is no choice over whether to exclude because of the school's anti-social behaviour agenda. An officer said that 'schools' policies are about punishment fitting the crime, with permanent exclusion as the ultimate sanction; they don't find out why the pupils behave as they do' and saw 'no reason' why the LA's figures should be higher than the national average.

Causes	Current responses
Pupil behavioural issues	With serious one-off incidents there is a move to immediate exclusion
Stated that behaviour has to change otherwise there is no choice but to exclude	Continuous disruption – seen to be more difficult to deal with – strategies include:
Behaviour leading to exclusions includes:	☐ use of internal exclusion room
☐ one-off incidents	☐ managed moves and hard to place protocol
☐ continuous disruption	☐ alternative provision for those at risk of permanent exclusion
Pupils travelling in from poor neighbourhoods in adjacent LAs	☐ placement of behavioural mentors in class
Difficult to engage parents in schools, especially when the school was not one of their top five choices.	☐ use of respite provision
	☐ VCS (*seen as an area for development*)
Schools are against/feel it is wrong to use their own money to deal with at risk children	Social and Emotion Aspects of Learning (SEAL) programme (*new development*)
Lack of co-ordinated support/multi-agency working,	School X has a behaviour protocol which is rigorously followed before a permanent exclusion can be issued. The protocol is embedded throughout the school with various levels and interventions to reduce the possibility of exclusion
Need for holistic package that includes family	
Lack of EPs	
	Mentoring offered as an alternative form of parenting [checking homework etc]
	Part-time timetable
Transitions	First six weeks in Year 7 spent in tutor group and provision of nurture group
For some at-risk/vulnerable children the move to secondary school can mean a lack of continuity of support that they have previously received leading to a culmination of issues building to a major incident	Accompanying some transitions are personal development plans and peer mentoring
	Primary learning mentors/SENCo follow up in secondary placement
Primary school example: can offer extensive package of support involving parents and identifying child needs at an early stage. This information is passed on to the secondary school but same support package may not be offered/available.	SEAL
	Assertive Discipline Policy
	After-school and lunchtime clubs
	BIP transition workers (*BIP schools only*)
	LEA produced pack to audit practice and policy around transitions
Incidents outside school either on way to school or from school [buses etc] – product of 'travel to school' factors including certain schools 'creaming off' pupils; leads to school/their pupils not being linked into community.	School 'patrols'
	Strategic development underway in LA concerning school catchment and placement

Table 4.9: perceived causes of exclusion and reported responses

The causes were located in the 'LA tradition' where schools went grant maintained in large numbers and animosity and mistrust set in between schools and between the school and the LA. 'Nurturing is not synonymous with this LA', it was said, and 'the schools are largely autonomous in the way they operate'.

Some headteachers had a very clear line on exclusions and the reasons for its use. The blame was located almost completely with the young people themselves.

> Headteacher: 'Reducing exclusions per se is not the game I want to play... but reducing the need for exclusion is ... I am not sure I want to 'drive' them [exclusions] down; I want attitudes and motivation to change'.

> Question: 'How do you improve attitude and behaviour? Whose job is that?'

> Headteacher: 'Not sure. That's the 64,000 dollar question. I suspect exclusions will fall when we can get more respect from the pupils. We want the behaviour to improve so it is not necessary'.

Another head said that in relation to the use of exclusions, 'it is not about raising the bar but about altering the children's behaviour'. Headteachers insisted that, 'all permanent exclusions have been an absolute last resort'. One head

---

Cameo: The resources allocated in one secondary school to social inclusion
The school has a relatively high deprivation intake with significant additional funding, including BIP money, in recognition of deprivation factors. It also has an accumulated budget surplus which is above the 5 per cent of the annual budget that is a recommended maximum from the DCSF. The school has organised a number of additional support mechanisms including a 5 A*-C booster room for Year 10s, an exclusion centre, a learning support unit and a nurture group.

The **5 A*- C booster room** was a hive of activity with 12 pupils, two teachers, computers, videos etc. There was a great deal of busyness, focus and teacher support on particular elements of work.

The **exclusion centre** was empty. This was a bare room only maintained in use three days a week.

The **nurture group** was empty on our arrival. A teacher arrived with one pupil. It was reported that the rest were absent.

The **learning support unit** was next door. It had no children in it.

The message is that funding is spent on boosting attainment levels. It is not spent on supporting the most needy or in setting up active preventative provision.

---

claimed that the view expressed at governors' reviews or at appeals panels was, 'We don't know how you held on to them for so long'.

It appears that some schools have become quite skilled in collating the evidence to substantiate the exclusion and to counter appeals. The means, internal to the school and external, are not well developed to support alternatives to exclusion. The last resort argument used to defend exclusion, common enough in secondary schools in every LA, is grossly unconvincing in LA 4.

Assets available

As an urban borough, the LA had available some city-wide initiatives and advice from multiple sources. It also had examples of schools which did not exclude excessively. Some assets are listed below.

- There are examples of secondary schools in LA 4 which do operate an inclusive ethos and have services and arrangements that mean they can and do continue to provide education for some quite challenging young people. The head of one said that they regarded it as a failure for them and a disaster for the pupil if they moved to a permanent exclusion. The school had taken six pupils in on reintegration agreements. Primary schools excluded at lower rates than the national average, which is commendable

- Fixed term exclusions have been maintained at a relatively low level

- LA 4 has the full range of agencies in place and talking to each other. The LA at senior level is acutely aware of its legal obligations and ensures that the LA is seen to fulfil these. It is an open authority, both in terms of providing data, documentation and information and in its willingness to call upon regional advisors to strategy meetings for addressing exclusion and behaviour issues

- The LA has a number of voluntary agencies which offer replacement education or in school support but these are allowed to function rather than being tied in to a LA strategy. Similarly, a directory of services had been produced listing all those who could be contacted for support in the locality but senior teachers using it had found it hard to reach such agencies and set up support packages; one (primary) headteacher had described needing stamina to keep chasing support and having to rely on a few organisations with which supportive relations had been established.

What is working

The LA has multiple initiatives but there are questions about ownership and embedding of practices. Items considered to be working in LA 4 are listed below.

- Mentoring and buddying schemes were regarded as having merit, along with restorative justice and mediation
- Building emotional intelligence – Social and Emotional Aspects of Learning (SEAL)
- Work on transitions
- Pupil at risk panel
- Identify needs and co-ordinate support
- Alternative provision at KS 4
- Easy identification of lead professional with links to external provisions
- Two new emerging positions will be filled soon for a NEET project officer and a KS 4 project officer which will be useful.

Clearly, these were not working effectively to reduce permanent exclusions from secondary schools in earlier years. It is uncertain if these can take credit for the reduction recorded in the last two years.

What is needed

In 2007/08, LA 4 secondary schools had an aggregate surplus of nearly £2 million. The recommended maximum surplus in secondary school is 5 per cent. Four schools had 5 per cent or more of their budgets unspent. These are resources which could and should be spent to address the deprivation issues for which they have been allocated. PRU costs in 2006/07 ran to £5.2 million, above the total annual budget of all but three of the authority's secondary schools. This appears to be funding that could be better spent and options should be examined. Indeed, one might ask if an exclusion should be allowed if the school can be shown to have money in its budget that could be allocated to the provision required for the pupil to be supported in continuing their education.

The charge levied from schools for exclusions above their quota, though appearing to be part of the reason for reduced exclusions at that time in 2007/08, could be seen as a repressive measure, unlikely to improve relationships with or practices in schools and was not an assured way to sustainably reduce exclusions.

To improve schools' capacity and structures, LA 4 needed some senior staff who are regular visitors to schools doing business with a small number of heads and senior school management to bring exclusion down, spend surpluses and make better and more flexible arrangements for inclusion. The levels of exclusion in LA 4 were extraordinarily high and are no doubt a cause for corporate embarrassment.

A *shift of culture is required* – a transformation in community awareness, which is characterised by a collaborative rather than a competitive ethos, with more trust, co-operation, and sharing. The LA would take on a new community role as a strategic partner, rather than be the predominant force.

Working with an existing informal alliance four secondary heads was a dramatic initiative suggested to the LA which would, in the project team's view, have precipitated the necessary cultural shift in LA 4. However, it was recognised that this option did not find favour. There are alternative routes which will achieve the same goal in a less abrupt, slower manner.

Relationships between schools and the LA have been damaged over the years. The project team found mistrust, resentment and contention between members of the education community. A restorative process is needed to enable all parties to draw a line under the past and open the way to a new beginning based upon a shared vision of community-based inclusion, with all parties committed to inclusive ideals and the collaborative model. Without the will to change, little can be achieved and the structures, however carefully constructed, will not function effectively.

A *coercive strategy will further alienate partners* and even if it is partially successful for a time it will be resented. Partners will continue to be obstructive and progress will be hindered and waylaid at every opportunity. Even change agent involvement can be ineffective, can indeed be used by the LA to suggest that it is drawing in advice and wisdom from far and wide and still the exclusion problem persists.

£5.2 million was spent on PRUs in 2006/07 and this could be reallocated to reprovision and multi-layer the system with groups or clusters of secondary schools. The main location for dealing with the young people is the school itself, with neighbouring schools as a resource and back up. While clusters and local partnerships are not well developed, informal groupings exist with the potential to develop collaborative arrangements. Concerns over crime, gangs, truancy, disaffection and NEET are best addressed where rejection is minimised and everyone counts.

It was stated that coordinated support and multi-agency working were needed – a holistic package including family work. There is a lack of EP support in LA 4. More PSHE was required at secondary school level and more multi-agency working, particularly outreach working with parents. One head reported, 'I don't recognise integrated children's services support in this authority'.

Project follow-up initiative
The project's work with LA 4 schools, officers and a range of other professionals sharpened understanding of the factors which push up exclusions and suggested constructive and collaborative ways of countering these. As part of the project's development work in LA 4, a plan was devised after consultation with four secondary headteachers who were on good terms informally. The goal was to improve the relationships, support schools in developing better internal arrangements for managing challenging pupils, eg with well staffed and well financed inclusion units, developing and co-ordinating better alternative education provision, working at developing managed moves and a revolving door PRU owned by this *ad hoc* cluster, all developed in what the schools would see as an equable and mutually supportive way. The shift in funding, control and responsibility for the cluster's most challenging children was central to the initiative. This radical plan would have been a demonstration project, bringing about a huge change in the embedded practices of years to achieve a huge reduction in permanent exclusion.

A plan was devised with the four selected headteachers which would entail their being a pathfinder group possibly taking over a PRU (and the proportion of the funding that went with it) and using it and other means within and between their schools to manage inclusion. The presentation made to LA 4 is presented in compressed form below:

1. Strategy
- A business plan that delivers the protocol
- We need schools to own the business plan and want to deliver it
- Need business plan to deliver reduced exclusions and real change in the short term
- We need it to deliver comprehensive change in the medium term

2. The business plan
- Directorate approve business plan

- Person appointed to act as trusted, robust go-between with schools (head of EOTAS)
  - initially to act as change agent
  - medium term to manage development
- Focus on high excluders – initial move with 'friendship' group of heads
- Reconfigure financial allocation model
  - Head of EOTAS to hold 1:1 discussions with each headteacher
  - establish a stakeholder forum for inclusion
  - key fund-holding and decision-making group

3. Real change in the short term

- Focus on four key secondary schools where there is a friendship group of headteachers including highest excluder and one low excluder
- Make them an offer they can't refuse!
- Give them more money to keep children in mainstream
- Give them enough to pay for the services they need
- Schools and Head of EOTAS agree targets following discussion

4. Real change in the medium term

- Reduce number of PRUs and redesignate them as school cluster facilities
- Schools (clusters) to manage PRUs
- Place of academies and CTCs to be addressed
- Address resource issues collaboratively
- PRU resources reconfigured more effectively
- Head of EOTAS accountable for quality of alternative provision
- Develop greater diversity in alternative provision.

The proposal was put to the LA 4 strategic group on behaviour in Autumn 2007 but the Interim Senior Director, Children, Schools and Community judged that an *ad hoc* working arrangement with a small group of secondary heads would not be appropriate and that new structures were being put in place. The possibility remains to pursue a negotiated form of the original proposal with the new postholders and work through new structures with an agenda that addresses the need for reconciliation, builds solidarity between partners, and opens the way to agreeing the terms of a new charter, in a way that will see it implemented. The above proposal was a multi-faceted, cross-school initiative that had prospects of breaking the mould.

Likelihood of success in reducing permanent exclusions by half
Responses were pessimistic: 'no chance', 'slim', 'extremely unlikely (laugh)' but also 'figures may improve as more people are interested'.

Type of provisions to address exclusions	Use *and* effectiveness of this provisions	How important could its role be 5 – 1	How important is its role currently 5 – 1
Inclusion units in schools	Only 6 in LA 4. Used as stepping stone to exclusion. Ineffective.	5	1
Alternative curriculum provision	Lots in IFP prog. Most alternative provision sourced by PRUs	*5*	*2*
Behaviour support (BIP, BEST etc.)	None provided external to school	5	1
Integrated multi-agency provision including VCS involvement	Vol Organisations involved in 'respite' and mentoring. Social services and CAMHS overwhelmed	*4, 5*	*2*
Focus on family and community support	Good at School A and other inclusive schools. Other schools very isolated.	4, 5	1
Managed moves	Increasingly used but worried it just moves problem round	3	2
PRU with reintegration role	Only accessed on entry via permanent exclusion.	4	1
Training of mainstream school staff	Vital – schools currently do not give it as high a priority as should. Tends to be 'one off's'	5	2
Special school and out of authority placement	Used a lot in LA 4 but all full and difficult to access	1	1
Support for transition	Vital – really important area. Some support via Connexions project and learning mentors but patchy	3	4

Table 4.10: Rating the potential and current importance of various types of service (5 is very important, 1 is of little or no importance) (one officer response)

Table 4.10 provides evidence of the judgement of one senior officer that the role of other agencies and initiatives in supporting the retention of children in schools was seriously inadequate. By contrast, ratings suggested that inclusion units, alternative curriculum BIP and BEST teams etc. could do a great deal. PRUs also have potential but, being full, could do no outreach work. Some statutory services were unable to respond in reasonable timescales and there were said to be very few alternative curriculum provision options outside the school

Review of success in reducing exclusions

Permanent exclusions have fallen in the last two years to a rate of 0.16 per cent, 'no longer pariah status in the exclusions league'. Fixed term exclusions have continued to be lower than the national average, and have fallen further still in 2007/08.

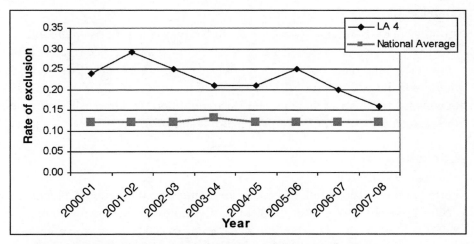

Figure 4.9: Permanent exclusion rates – LA 4 and England

An officer said that the charging regime re-established in Autumn 2007 has been the main reason for the reduction in permanent exclusions. This is to be followed up with support for the schools but resources, relationships and skills will need to be in place for this to happen.

A headteacher perspective, more in evidence in LA 4 than in the others, was that the problem lay with pupil behaviour; exclusions would drop, it was argued, when behaviour and respect improved. An inclusive authority is one where there is a critical mass consensus that schools have a significant duty to adjust and create provision to meet the needs of all. Additionally, the LA would have supportive services and dialogue would be open, robust and con-

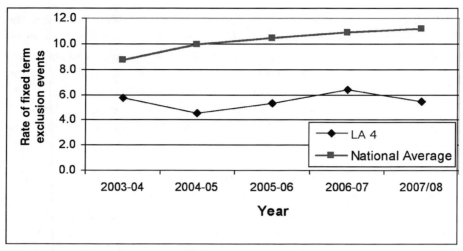

Figure 4.10: Secondary school fixed term exclusion rates – LA 4 and England

structive in casework and provision for individuals and groups vulnerable to exclusion. The force comes from LA Members backing senior officers who negotiate with those who manage schools to establish cost effective arrangements for the education of pupils at risk of exclusion. If this develops, the downward trend in exclusions can be maintained, children will continue their education and NEET groups will diminish in size.

Local authority 5 (LA 5)

Preliminary analysis

Permanent exclusions in LA 5 rose from a little over the national average in 2000/01, reaching one and a half times the national rate before falling in 2005/06 – but to a level distinctly above the rate in 2000. The reason appeared to be systemic or an outcome of intolerance by the professional community.

LA 5 has over 500 primary schools and over 100 secondary schools and a pupil population of over 150,000. There were 260 secondary school exclusions in 2005/06. Thirteen secondary schools excluded six or more pupils in 2005/06, 41.5 per cent of the total. LA 5 excludes KS 4 pupils at a higher rate than the national average. This is said to be because of the lack of alternative provision.

Whilst LA 5 has the usual variation in levels of deprivation, and exclusions tend to be concentrated in areas with the most challenging socio-economic characteristics, the pattern of exclusions seems to be both high and unstable. During the 18 months the project worked alongside LA 5, dramatic changes occurred in levels of exclusion. Were the problem limited to a few high deprivation, high excluding schools where specific services needed to be put in and support provided, the task would be easier. Had there been tensions and battles between the local authority at its centre or in the areas and the schools, then again a solution could be identified. But neither situation applied.

There are moderate negative correlations (approximately -0.48) between secondary school attainment and exclusions, permanent and fixed term; high exclusion rates are moderately strongly related to low levels of attainment. There is also a moderately high correlation between fixed term and permanent exclusion which had been fairly stable over the previous three years in both the primary and secondary sectors. This suggests that there is a general exclusionary force at work.

There is some consistency in rates of exclusion over the years, some of the areas into which the LA is divided regularly having higher rates than others. The spread is quite striking, varying in 2005/06 in secondary permanent exclusions from a low of 0.08 per cent in one area to a high of 0.6 per cent in another (national average 0.24%). LA 5 has been a high permanent excluding authority for a number of years. It stands at the bottom of the highest quartile of excluders and because of its large number of schools contributes significantly to the national total. The research team interviewed many different stakeholders in the wider domain of children and young people care and development, focusing increasingly on schools to get reactions to the pressures pushing exclusions up and the services to help keep them down. In the last phase, the focus was on the historically highest excluding area.

Reasons for high rates of exclusion
The high numbers of both permanent and fixed term exclusions, particularly from the secondary schools, are a cause for concern. There appears to be general consensus about the reasons for such high rates of exclusion. Most obvious is the exclusion culture that prevailed within schools. It seems that 'every school has its own policies', that 'schools act in isolation', and that there exists a distinct 'lack of consistency and diverse levels of tolerance and inclusiveness among schools'. Zero tolerance is a significant factor, where the one-off incident is the trigger for exclusion. There is a lack of mutual understanding amongst the many agencies that provide support to schools, which reduces the effectiveness of interactions between them.

Specific reasons for the high numbers of exclusions were given:

- No robust mechanism exists which can challenge decisions to exclude
- Delegation of behaviour funding streams to independent organisations and agencies
- No training on how do deal with difficult behaviour
- Little induction or training for governors, heads and teaching staff regarding exclusions and promotion of alternative solutions
- Head left with no other option but to exclude – eg difficult child at high risk in a school not resourced to deal with them appropriately. 'The headteacher must be seen to punish unacceptable behaviour' and 'the head can be under pressure from teaching staff to exclude'
- Exclusion meetings are not attended by professionals working in the field of social support but by clerks, administrators etc
- 50 per cent of aided schools do not buy in to LA governor services
- Pressures to meet targets set by LA and national government on attainment and expectations of acceptable behaviour
- Lack of awareness of what alternative solutions exist – a lack of networking and partnerships
- Lack of joint planning such that services are working in isolation and some agencies work faster than others
- No common understanding of the concept 'at risk children and families' and a belief that a 'fantasy provision' exists which has the resources to cope with high risk children
- Lack of nurturing provision throughout and a perceived need for CAMHS services.

Assets available

Provision within the schools is variable and the good practice pursued by some headteachers could profitably be disseminated amongst all schools.

- Behaviour management training has been very successful in some schools, providing teachers with helpful and efficient skills, which in turn leads to enhanced confidence in the classroom and boosts morale amongst the staff
- Counselling and mentoring in the learning situation are strongly recommended in some schools, and pastoral support is available.
- Youth and community services are actively engaged in support for schools with behavioural problems

■ The LA provides support services for schools including the EPs and EWOs, who are effectively engaged and have a lot of experience in this field

■ The Behaviour Support Centre provides an effective service for schools, and according to one headteacher has 'reduced our fixed term exclusions'

■ The PRUs themselves have a positive self-image and in many cases provide behaviour management training for teachers in the schools. They also provide support in schools with advice, particularly when the schools contact them to seek support. This is more likely to occur with Primary Schools, where 'the majority of heads do not want to exclude and will refer to the PRU in the early stages'. According to the PRU headteacher, one third of pupils coming into the PRU could have been kept in school had the staff had appropriate training

■ The LA has produced a document on alternative curriculum providers which lists almost 100. The fact that one head wished for more alternative curricula seems to support the view that 'heads don't know the range of services available to them'

■ An account of current provision for behaviour support in 2006 stated that 'over 90 different services offer specialist input in addition to what individual schools and other educational settings provide'. They include Connexions, CAMHS, LEMS, GRIP and YIP

■ FE colleges provide some courses more appropriate to many pupils classed as disaffected in schools

■ The YOT can be helpful but is probably underused. Managed transfer can be helpful, and there is a hard-to-place protocol in existence.

What is working

Clearly, across a large authority, many things will be working. The challenge is to disseminate and embed the best that is known to operate locally in supporting challenging young people. Some of the elements that work well in some parts of the LA are listed below.

■ Some headteachers do not exclude permanently and show that, with a judicious use of fixed term exclusions and giving other support, they can manage all their pupils. One headteacher, who has not permanently excluded since 2004, states, 'Every time I exclude it is an admission of defeat, and permanent exclusion is a huge defeat'

- Continuing professional development which includes behaviour management training has proved to be most effective in equipping teachers with skills needed to cater for all their pupils and at the same time boosting their confidence
- The appointment of attendance officers enhances the relationship between home and school and allows the school to understand the family as a whole. It helps the school to appreciate the situation of the pupil and adds a whole new dimension with which to inform the strategy to pursue in order to provide for the needs of the pupil. This relationship also allows the pupil and parents to have a voice which will be listened to with respect, with the intention of strengthening the bond and carrying the family along with the strategy to help the pupil.

Secondary school cameo – the broadened community school remit

The headteacher of this secondary school introduced a raft of measures designed to manage and maintain *all* pupils in the school. There was a need to deal with offending pupils and to bolster the morale and confidence amongst the staff. He devised a Teaching and Learning and Behaviour Discipline Policy, distributed to all parties, including parents, which was very prescriptive. The teachers have received a great deal of support and training for behaviour management. He appointed two attendance officers who have made 2,500 home visits in $2^1/_2$ years. They involve the parents in the work and behaviour of their children in the school and will bring them into school to meet teachers and drop them off at work if necessary. He set up an *Every Child Matters Centre* and combined the separate Success Maker Unit and SEN, which every pupil will access during their school career. Both counselling and mentoring are considered highly significant within the school. There is a Reading Recovery Programme for Year 7 pupils with a reading age of < 9.7. The school makes use of the Educational Medical Service and CAMHS, the EWS and Social Services, and a time-out service for KS 3 and 4.

Competitions are held regularly to increase the levels of attendance such as the Grand National. Each class owns a horse and there are hurdles to jump. Each weekly hurdle requires a class attendance of 91 per cent and each hurdle is sponsored by a local company, which produces the prizes for the ultimate winners at the end of six weeks.

The headteacher has not permanently excluded a pupil since 2004. 'The rationale is to stop seeing children as 'problems' and to begin to appreciate their needs within a caring, inclusive culture'.

■ On-site Behaviour Support Centres are extremely useful in moments of stress and provide a convenient time-out provision for both pupil and teacher. Managed moves, already established and recommended, are working well when required, and have scope for further refinement

■ The FE colleges offering alternative courses play a major role in providing for disaffected pupils and there is a genuine call for more provision of this nature. Colleges report that the attendance of the pupils on their courses is very high, although it was abysmal in mainstream schools

■ The Behaviour Support Centres make a valuable contribution, and for one head the centre has significantly reduced fixed term exclusions.

The secondary school described in the cameo demonstrated much that is needed to accommodate the full range of young people. It had determinedly and imaginatively broadened its provision.

What is needed
There is a real need for a change in schools of hearts and minds, for the wholehearted adoption of an appropriate culture that will encompass all the pupils in the school. For every child to matter, nothing less will do. Classroom management is a significant part of the strategy to ensure ownership of pupils, and many schools need help with this. Conveniently, help is never far away. As one PRU head put it: 'With co-operation, there is so much more we could do to support schools'.

According to some headteachers, the referral system can be chaotic, and there is a need for better response mechanisms to be available at earlier stages. On the other hand, many providers despair at the lack of early intervention, and describe the call for their involvement as arriving at the crisis stage. The LA can act as broker, monitor, organiser and quality assurer with the support services

Supportive services, including EPs, EWOs, CAMHS, YOT, GRIP, Connexions and Social Services, need to improve the range of their support for schools. It is clearly evident that each service operates independently from the others, with its own internal culture. Many comments refer to the shortcomings of other services and there is demand for better quality services, better attendance at multi-agency meetings, and more professional discussions with schools, rather than rushed, *ad hoc* conversations only when problems have escalated. Multi-agency working in the context of schools is a reality, but a joined-up, integrated, communicating multi-agency service remains embryonic. Yet it is the key to resolving most of the current problems.

Many pupils find mainstream schooling a turn-off, and completely irrelevant to their needs and interests. An alternative curriculum can transform their attitude and behaviour, and attendance then improves. The schools need to look more carefully at this route for pupils whose disaffection with standard provision is so strong.

Project follow-up initiative

Discussions with the steering group and the Head of Inclusion led to the decision to focus on Area A, the high excluding area of the LA. This was a high deprivation area and the KS 3 PRU was on a 'renowned' estate. Permanent exclusions across the LA for the autumn term 2007 had increased hugely over the previous year's figures. A striking development too had been in the numbers of primary school exclusions which, for the Autumn term 2007, already exceed the total for the whole of 2006/07. However, quite remarkably, permanent secondary exclusions in the previously high excluding area were reduced and at the current rate would be lower than in 2006/07 (0.35 compared with 0.45%) while the other two areas came close to doubling their area permanent exclusion rates.

The secondary schools in the area are much disrupted with school amalgamations and the Building Schools for the Future programme; the latter is not running to time. Local partnerships are operating and there is a hard to place protocol operating. The pupil referral service does not get high marks from one headteacher, but the KS 4 PRU was described as 'like a breath of fresh air. Brilliant'. This headteacher sent staff to the PRU for staff development and they have had transition mentors operating with external funding, from whom much could be learned.

In Area A, the KS 3 PRU opened in September 2007, replacing a previous PRU which had been 'a dumping ground'. There had been a gap of one term when there had been greatly reduced PRU provision. The PRU deals with 11 secondary schools and offers 32 full time and 20 respite and intervention places although the hope was that there would be more outreach with intervention. The PRU opened with 'a glut of permanent exclusions' (was 31 now 21) and many had been out for some while. This PRU does not exclude and is complemented by the KS 4 PRU which, although there are 'lifers', is said to work very well. The PRU headteacher has money for temporary staff to go out to school and some school staff are being trained along with PRU staff to spread the expertise. She would like her centre to accommodate no more than 10 permanently excluded pupils. She has promoted the Alternative Curriculum and the message for schools is: if she has done it in her centre, 'so can you'. She urged that one had to look for the strengths in young people. She has built up a diversity of contacts and said that schools could access these.

The KS 3 PRU was headed by a senior person in the LA who had considerable authority. She had responsibility locally for the PRU but also for multi-agency panel meetings which are held at six weekly intervals. They are attended by a whole range of professionals, including an advisor who is a School Improvement Partner (SIP).

She says that the role of one significant LA person in the area is crucial and requires being 'not threatening but demanding'. The PRU head has been into schools where the LSUs were being planned and advised. There needs to be help for secondary school units on how to set them up and how to manage them most effectively.

At the multi-agency meetings, every child in the PRU is discussed. There is a recording template with an 'Action' column and an 'Outcome'. At the next meeting the staff are challenged and they do this for all the children at each of the three 'Short Term Schools'. If representatives do not come, she emails. She informs them of the outcome so they get the work anyway. She is strict about the paperwork. It has to be done.

The head of the PRU insists that schools must phone if on the verge of excluding. 'I will get back to them. I will have an alternative – there is always an alternative to excluding'. When this early warning convention is bypassed she will contact the school, ask why they had not made contact before. Whatever the explanation given, she asserts, 'No, you should have rung me'. Where things do not go quite right, 'we have had quite a few conversations'.

While it is difficult to attribute the downturn in permanent exclusion numbers to one person or even the collection of PRU heads, it does seem that the combination of robust engagement with schools coupled with the offers of solutions works – for the schools and the young people.

Likelihood of success in reducing exclusions by half
The responses to the question about halving permanent exclusions were pessimistic. To succeed in this by 2006/7 was considered 'not good' at best, although one felt it was a 'yes' for primary schools. By 2007/8 there was some chance of such a reduction, but not for the secondary schools.

The central co-ordinating role for the management of behaviour and inclusion in a large authority is clearly a requirement. Data and intelligence must be monitored at the centre so that fast changing needs and circumstances are responded to appropriately. Clear documentation and guidance also needs to be co-ordinated at that level and this is impressively done. This support from the LA centre might not be complemented by the necessary challenge and co-working on exclusions eg through SIPs or National Strategy consultants.

The management of funds for excluded pupils needs to be carefully examined to ascertain whether it provides value for money in terms of the outputs at the end but also, and more importantly, to see whether supporting pupils in schools or other forms of alternative provision may put them in a better position for moving on from Key Stage 4 to education training or employment even to gain better qualifications at GCSE Level. It cannot be emphasised too much that PRUs are expensive, usually costing more than three times the amount spent per secondary pupil in a mainstream school. One consequence of this knowledge is that it invites the question for headteachers, PRU heads and others in the district about whether that money could be better used in providing for the pupils. They might decide, individually or collectively, not to spend three times the pupil cost to manage their challenging pupils and that there is a good business case for maintaining them in the school.

In an Every Child Matters sense, this involves the employment of new staff such as family link workers, counsellors, mentors, to support children in schools, in addition to having learning support units, inclusion centres etc. What is needed are alternative curriculum developments and support for their use, and referrals to them. FE Colleges have a role to play here but they generally are reluctant to increase numbers significantly – unless some special deals can be done. Managed moves, already established and recommended in LA 5, could be further developed and the funding and support requirements, both from within and outside the school, further scrutinised.

LA 5 has a number of impressive instances of schools operating multi-layered support facilities which appear to work in maintaining young people in school and keeping them on track to qualifications and a successful transition to the next stage. With the movement toward extended schools, careful costing of these additional facilities might show that there are greater possibilities than we currently are aware of for schools to extend their capacities to manage challenging pupils. There is a constant need to exhort headteachers to think inclusively and to understand the consequences for education and other services when a pupil is excluded. New ways of allocating funding, possibly directly related to supporting a young person in school in a preventative fashion, could be developed further.

Type of provisions to address exclusions	Use *and* effectiveness of this provisions	How important *could* its role be	How important *is* its role currently
Inclusion units in schools		5, 5, 4, 3/4	5, 3/4
Alternative curriculum provision	*Note providers (school, VCS, FE, private)*	*5, 5, 5, 4/5*	*5, 2, 2*
	Note scale of operation, pupil numbers		
Behaviour support (BIP, BEST etc.)		5, 5, 5, 4/5	3, 3/4
Integrated multi-agency provision including VCS involvement	*List other agencies involved. List VCS involvement and its scale*	4, 5, 4	2, 2, 1
Focus on family and community support		5, 5, 3, 3/4	1, 5, 1
Managed moves		4, 2, 4, 5	1-5, 2, 1
PRU with reintegration role		5, 5, 5	5, 1
Training of mainstream school staff		5, 5, 5, 4/5	5, 5, 3
Special school and out of authority placement		5, 5, 5	5, 5, 5

Table 4.11: Rating the potential and current importance of various types of service (5 is very important, 1 is of little or no importance)

The difference in scores between what is currently working and how important the provision *could* be was in many cases considerable. Integrated multi-agency provision was generally seen as much less useful than it could be, as was the focus on family and community support and managed moves. Alternative curriculum provision was also lacking. Inclusion units in school were considered to be functioning at optimal level and training of mainstream school staff is ongoing, considered important and functioning at near its potential.

Review of progress in reducing exclusions
The exclusion statistics in LA 5 for the Autumn term 2007 alone showed some surprises. Because Area A was the highest excluder, our attention was directed towards the schools and services in this area. In the Autumn term of

2007, it was the *lowest* excluder and had shown quite dramatic falls in exclusions. Some of this can be explained by the recent history, such as the amalgamation of schools being completed, but it would seem to be also a product of energetic working between the PRU management and schools.

Fixed term exclusions were reducing most markedly in Area A too. This was true also of days lost, where again the greatest reduction was in this Area. During the course of the project's work with LA 5, a striking development – seen also in some of the other project LAs – was in the rise in primary school permanent exclusions. In the Autumn term 2007, these already exceeded the total for the whole of 2006/07.

The picture for the whole 2007/08 year from all of LA 5 was an increase in permanent exclusions but a large reduction in fixed term exclusion in the secondary schools.

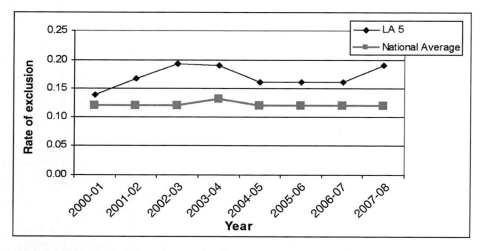

Figure 4.11: Permanent exclusion rates – LA 5 and England 2000 – 2008

Where there has been strong co-ordinated local decision-making about the management of challenging young people, this has clearly shown results. This requires liaison between schools and the Pupil Referral Unit. PRUs have to fight hard to keep numbers down so they can engage in outreach work and support within schools. At present, despite sound documentation and good intention, and even good relationships between local authority officers and headteachers, the assured, non-excluding management of challenging pupils is still difficult to achieve. It appears to require at local level or district level the co-ordinating strength of an influential (and possibly highly paid) individual

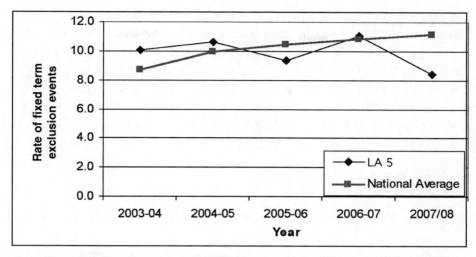

Figure 4.12: Secondary school fixed term exclusion rates – LA 5 and England 2003 – 2008

who can work with schools to drive down exclusions and is in a position to deliver small amounts of funding from the local authority or release funding which is saved by pupils not going into PRUs.

The views of parents and excluded pupils

Twelve parents were interviewed by telephone. All were the parents of boys who had been permanently excluded. Thirty two pupils were interviewed across the five LAs. All were secondary age and 27 of them were in PRUs. Confidentiality guarantees were given. The main messages are reported in condensed form under the headings below.

Parents are generally supportive of their children's education

All the parents were very supportive of their children in school. They appreciated the value of a good education and recognised whether or not a school was doing all it could to provide this. Most had a tale of woe to tell with regard to the level of support their children received from the school in times of need.

Parents try to be supportive of school efforts

Parents reported that they were willing to play their part in a co-ordinated effort with the school in order to manage their children's behaviour in school.

Acceptance that their children's behaviour was challenging

The challenging nature of behaviour presented by these children, often severe and generally quite frequent, was acknowledged by the parents. According to those interviewed, their sons conformed to the usual pattern of pupils who are permanently excluded due to behaviour regarded by the school as unacceptable. They were disruptive in the classroom, would wander around the school during lesson time, would be aggressive, argumentative and often used bad language.

Schools unhelpful

Parents claimed that the school failed to play its part:

> I went to the school many times to explain things, like a time-out card, but the teachers didn't seem to want to know.

> Simply shouting at a slightly deaf ADHD pupils doesn't work at all (mother of a bright boy with hearing difficulties and ADHD).

> He wanted to work but the teachers wouldn't help him.

> Simple strategies, like positioning pupils with hearing difficulties at the front of the class, were not followed. Secondary schools, it was said, 'didn't want to know', 'would not bend' or were 'simply not doing their job'.

Parents' proposals for alternatives to exclusion included 'a special unit, a time-out card, and a special teacher to turn to', 'more support and understanding'. However, one set of parents acknowledged that they 'couldn't think of any more the school could have done'.

Insufficient strategies employed by schools for pupils displaying challenging behaviour

Support for difficult pupils appeared to be limited. One school only had a 'detention centre' with no support or mentoring of any kind. Another had a 'special behaviour unit' which did not sound like a place providing support. Yet another had an 'isolation unit' with a teacher 'nearby'. 'Someone took him boxing once, and although a mentor was promised, he never materialised'.

Some schools were reported to appreciate the need for agreeing a plan of action with the parents, agreed a plan to manage difficult behaviour, but failed to follow the procedures when these were required most. 'Promises made but never kept' as one despairing mother described it. Parents frequently referred to schools as 'not friendly, not supportive' – even 'hostile'.

The exception to this negative picture concerned one pupil who hated his secondary school when he transferred from primary and made every effort to be excluded because his friends transferred to a different secondary school. School support was immense and the parents said that, 'The school couldn't have done more to keep him in; they simply ran out of options'.

Impact on parents

One parent said that her son was 'badly affected' by his exclusion, depressed because he 'missed his mates', but 'happy to be away from the bullying teachers'. The effect on his mother was also deeply disturbing:

> It was a big thing at the time, everything happened all at once, I was depressed with it all, plus pressure from the school ringing up every day.

Placement in the PRU

Parents reported for the most part that their children enjoyed their PRU; they liked the curriculum, got on well with the teachers and made plenty of friends. The parents found it 'completely different' from school, with 'plenty of contact', 'very supportive, friendly and helpful'. Pupils at the PRU reported positive relationships with staff at the PRU, unlike 'the uncooperative teachers in mainstream schools'. Pupils praised the PRU and enjoyed the range of provision.

Pupils' views on their behaviour

Two Year 8 pupils had been permanently excluded in the last year for serious incidents such as carrying a knife and hitting a teacher. Both acknowledged the seriousness of these offences. Two pupils had received some form of support such as a mentor or transition worker, which they described as 'helpful but not helpful enough' and 'a bit helpful'.

Some of the excluded pupils interviewed did not think that the exclusion had been unwarranted, 'Too many appearances in too many things, seclusion unit about 50 times, they reached the end of their tether'. They seemed to realise that their behaviour had put them into a position where the school might take this decision. One pupil from Year 10 even saw benefits from having been excluded, 'Good thing I was expelled. It sorted me out a lot. I would have been worse'.

School issues

All the pupils had been permanently excluded, and all but one – who had none had – experienced up to four fixed term exclusion. The reason for permanent exclusions included serious offences such as violence or carrying a knife, but in the main it was for a build up of 'too many things' – a catalogue of incidents over a period of a year and in some cases years. Three pupils interviewed in a secondary school were referred to an inclusion centre based in the school and had received one to one support from the centre.

Two PRU based pupils reported struggling at school; a boy found his lessons difficult and 'boring' and a girl reported disruption to her school life because of her anti-social behaviour at weekends. Alcohol abuse and disorderly behaviour were also reported, as well as social services involvement with her family. Only one child interviewed had been excluded for a specific one-off incident, and most described the lead up to the exclusion as a 'build up of past incidents'. Some were critical of the schools; others thought the school could not have done anything else.

Reintegration
Many pupils recalled having lots of friends at school and said they missed them. Most were appreciative of the support they received and the relationships they had established in the PRUs/Diversity. Some expressed the wish to stay there. However, the majority, even the Year 10s, wanted to go back to mainstream secondary school.

General findings across all parents and excluded pupils
Whilst many of the parents might report in an unbalanced way, the negative attitudes and practices of schools which they describe contrast with the relationships with and support from the PRUs the pupils experienced. The widespread inability to handle a shared problem in a calm and constructive way in which the parents and school staff work towards a shared goal is certainly cause for concern.

The majority of pupils did not particularly dislike school and seemed to be experiencing behaviour difficulties to a varying extent. Only a few reported severe behavioural or learning difficulties. Almost all pupils reported negative relationships with all the teachers in mainstream school, except for the odd one or two with whom they could talk. But they described relationships with staff in PRUs positively.

Almost all pupils reported having no disruptions at home that might affect the way they behaved at school. The few who were experiencing problems at home had received some support from an outside agency. The involvement of outside agencies did not, however, figure prominently in the accounts given by the pupils or parents. Reintegration remains a challenge: long waits with no planned date for return to mainstream, with or without a package of support, are the common picture in LA 5.

School funding and deprivation allocations

The mean unit cost per pupil varied across the five LAs. LAs made annual Section 52 financial returns in a common format to the DCSF and figures set out in Table 4.12 were derived from these returns. These took the Age Weighted Pupil Unit (AWPU) of costing and added all the other funds received by the school for special needs, deprivation factors, ethnicity and second language learners etc.

The secondary school additions in one large LA (LA 5) varied from 10 per cent to 85 per cent on top of the initial pupil numbers and unit cost calculation. Different LAs have different formulae but the underlying rationale is that schools facing greater challenges should receive more money per pupil. The table below gives the mean and the highest and lowest in each LA. In LA 3's secondary school budget, between 13.6 per cent and 22.2 per cent of school budgets are additional beyond the AWPU.

Local Authority	Mean secondary unit cost per pupil	Highest	Lowest	% range
LA 1	£5765	£7750	£4532	71.0%
LA 2	£4579	£5479	£4017	36.4%
LA 3	£4180	£4693	£3947	18.9%
LA 4	£5090	£6517	£4463	46.0%
LA 5	£5041	£6862	£33819	79.7%

Table 4.12: Pupil Unit costs 2006/07

Much of the additional funding is deprivation money for schools to use to address the additional social and educational needs which their school is calculated to have. The DCSF is enquiring into the extent to which this funding is being appropriately targeted. The project's experience in various schools is that this additional formula-driven funding is not targeted at areas for which this money is intended.

Whilst the differential might need reconsideration, even an increase, the money which moves with the challenging young person might be at higher levels – or even be money used to ensure retention of a pupil. Greater delegation to school clusters in the three areas might be worth pursuing if tied to an assured responsibility for continued education of at risk children.

Additionally, some schools have built up surpluses. The DCSF recommendation is that surpluses should be no greater than 5 per cent in secondary schools and 8 per cent in primary schools. The object is that the money should be spent on the pupils currently in the school. There were a number of secondary schools where the percentage surplus exceeded this. The collective sum in an LA might be quite large and could be directed to areas of need speedily.

Certainly, where there are high levels of need, one would expect deprivation allocations to be targeted at pupils with low attainment and challenging behaviour and that surpluses in schools where these problems are most obvious would be spent on addressing these issues – and not remain in banks.

The pupil premium, payable from September, 2011, at the rate of £430 per pupil, increases the differential in funding. There is more explicit pressure to see this additional funding allocated to initiatives to address low attainment and high exclusions of those in 'deprived circumstances'.

5

Outcomes

The short term impact

The action project could claim modest success in the short term. Permanent exclusions fell in the five local authorities between 2003/04, the counting period prior to the project, and 2007/08 when the project was completed. Fixed term exclusions actually increased in two of the LAs and in the overall total, though three of the LAs actually reduced the number of recorded instances during this period. Where the biggest falls occurred it was clear that officers and schools had worked well together to develop new forms of provision and new agreements about the management and transfer of challenging young people. In large local authorities the problems are greater because of

Objective	Performance indicator	Outcome November 2008
1. Reductions in exclusion within the five LAs in Year 1 and Year 2 of the project compared with the 2003/04 baseline.	50% reduction in permanent exclusion; 30% reduction in fixed term exclusions (July 2008).	Average 30% reduction in permanent exclusions comparing 2003/04 with 2007/08 5% reduction in FT exclusion compared with the national rising rate
2. Better provision, higher achievement levels and greater inclusion for at risk young people.	Fewer young people out of education or on the hard to place list (20% reduction – July 2008).	Numbers out of mainstream have not altered Acknowledgement of personalised learning and a broadening of what is legitimate alternative provision

Objective	Performance indicator	Outcome November 2008
3. A fuller understanding at local level of the forces behind high levels of exclusion and the needs of at-risk young people and their families who may be subject to exclusion.	LA officers and stakeholders registering their greater understanding Young people and their families feeling that their needs are being better heard, understood and met.	Officers have huge local knowledge and are busy – unsure if the project has contributed to their understanding
4. Processes and tools tailored to their context to tackle exclusions.	LA officers and stakeholders acknowledging appreciation of the tools.	The tools are available on web: http://www.gre.ac.uk/__data/assets/pdf_file/0016/511630/res rcs-alternative-tools.pdf
5. Practical recommendations and guidance on managing pupils at risk of exclusion using multi-agency approaches including the VCS and operating with supportive and restorative principles.	Recommendations and guidance produced.	Four side circular to LAs. This document, national conference (2009 four regional workshops July 2010-May 2011)
6. Criteria of good practice in the management of exclusions.	Criteria produced.	See chapter 6
7. A fully documented account of the developmental work with the five action sites, support documentation, action planning.	Documented account produced	This book

Table 5.1: Objectives, performance indicators and outcomes of the project

the difficulty of a focus on a limited number of schools where relationships can be established, deals done and new arrangements set out. The objectives, performance indicators and outcomes are as set out in Table 5.1 above.

The permanent exclusion rates shown in Figure 5.1 are official DfES/DCSF/DfE ones, with the national average for 2009/10 being an extrapolation of the trend to accompany the LAs' own reports on 2009/10 exclusions. Three of the five LAs showed a significant decline in their rates of permanent exclusion between Time 1 and Time 2. All were on a downward trend in the last two years except LA 5. LA 2 was particularly impressive in actually bringing its rate to under half the national rate. LA 5 was set on a 'plateau' rather higher than the national average with signs that it would come lower – and one of its areas did – but over all saw a return to the 2003/04 level.

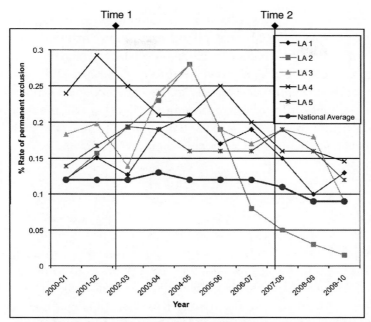

Note: the National Average exclusion rate for 2009/10 is an estimated trend extrapolation

Figure 5.1: Permanent exclusions in five LAs compared with national average

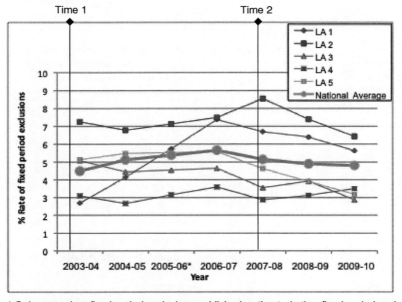

* Only secondary fixed period exclusions published; estimated other fixed period exclusions added

Figure 5.2: Fixed term secondary school exclusions in the five LAs compared with national average

Fixed term exclusions were on a steady increase nationally up to 2006/07. Three of the project LAs reduced fixed period exclusions, including one (which had been the highest permanent excluder in 2003/04) which retained a below average rate of officially recorded fixed term exclusions. With the development of inclusion centres in schools, a minority of secondary schools used these as substitutes for fixed term exclusion, recognising that the time off school usually meant that pupils, who were not generally on top of their work, would get even further behind; an achievement model prevailed.

The longer term impact

Figures 5.1. and 5.2 also show the two year period after the project ended. The momentum for decreases continued through to 2010 though only LA2 continued its remarkable reduction in permanent exclusions. Three others continued a downward trend. Fixed period exclusion rates reduced in all the LAs except for LA4 which nonetheless remained a below average fixed period excluder. In terms of permanent exclusions it would seem that only LA2 had accomplished the 'step change', and then managed to extend and consolidate prevention work. However, although across LAs generally high permanent exclusions go with high fixed period exclusions, LA 2 was the highest fixed period excluder and its network of PRUs had relatively high populations.

Local Authority	No. of permanent exclusions 2003/04	No. of young people benefiting by reduction			No. of fixed period exclusions 2003/04	No. of young people benefiting by reduction (- indicates an increase)		
		50% reduction target	Reduct-ion 2007/08	Reduct-ion 2009/10		30% reduct-ion target	Reduct-ion 2007/08	Reduct-ion 2009/10
LA 1	330	165	69	117	7,130	2,139	-4,480	-2,642
LA 2	50	25	43	46	1,540	462	-170	269
LA 3	40	20	11	25	650	195	100	210
LA 4	110	55	36	37	1,530	459	90	-241
LA 5	330	165	9	121	9,010	2,703	1,420	3,856
Total	860	430	168	346	19,860	5,958	-3,040	1,452
National Totals	9,880				344,510			

Table 5.2: Permanent and fixed period exclusions and reduction targets for 2007/08 and outcomes in 2009/10 in the five high excluding LAs

Table 5.2 below gives the number of young people who, it was calculated, would directly benefit from their LA's participation in the project. The figures are based on the LAs' permanent and fixed term exclusion rates from 2003/ 04. The aim had been that 430 fewer young people would be permanently excluded and there would be nearly 6,000 fewer fixed period exclusions by 2007/08. In the event, 168 fewer were excluded permanently. The total number of fixed period exclusions in the five LAs increased, even though three had managed to reduce their rates.

During this period nationally, permanent exclusion fell to 8,680 (2006/07 figure), a reduction of 12%. Fixed period exclusions increased enormously to 363,980, which may be partly because of better recording. This amounted to a 28% increase. Three LAs reduced fixed term exclusions, LA 1 actually exceeded the national rate of increase, but LA 2 was slightly below it. By 2009/01, the numbers had reduced to those nearer the targets. Table 5.3 shows the reductions by 2007/08 and 2009/10 relative to their numbers in 2003/04 and relative to the national reduction.

In terms of permanent exclusions, four of the five LAs reduced exclusions in 2007/08 by a greater proportion than the national average; by 2009/10 the average reduction across the five significantly exceeded the fairly impressive national reduction. The national figure had reduced to 6,550, equating to 0.9% of the school population. Fixed period exclusions had increased nationally over the 2003/04 levels but by 2009/10 overall, the project LAs had actually achieved a reduction.

LA	Permanent exclusions		Fixed period exclusions	
	% reductions in permanent exclusions 2007/08	% reductions in permanent exclusions 2009/10	% reductions in fixed period exclusions 2007/08	% reductions in fixed period exclusions 2009/10
LA 1	20.9%	35.5%	-62.8%	-37.1%
LA 2	86.0%	92.0%	-11.0%	17.5%
LA 3	27.5%	62.5%	15.4%	32.3%
LA4	32.7%	33.6%	5.9%	-15.8%
LA 5	2.7%	36.7%	15.8%	42.8%
Total	19.5%	40.2%	-15.3%	7.3%
National rates of increase/decrease	17.2%	33.7%	-11.4%	-5.4%

Table 5.3: Reductions in exclusions in five high excluding LAs from 2003/4 base

To press home the point about the LA dynamic that must be harnessed to reduce exclusions, it is helpful to return to the three low excluding cases used as a starting point in the quest for strategies to promote inclusion. Figure 5.3

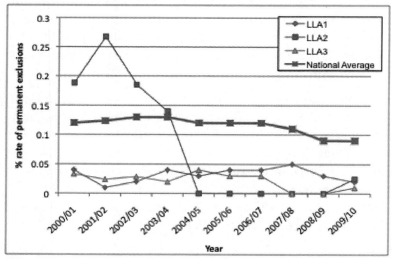

Figure 5.3: Permanent exclusions in three low excluding LAs compared with national average

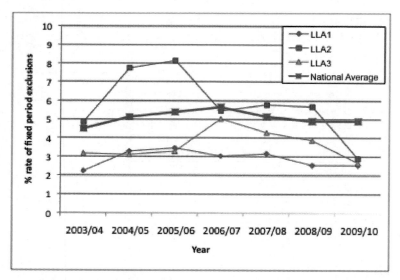

Figure 5.4: Fixed term exclusions in three low excluding LAs compared with the national average

shows that they remained very low excluders, way below the national rates. It had become accepted practice and these officers and headteachers continue strategies and practices that work for them.

In terms of fixed period exclusions, they have clearly worked hard at reducing the rates of exclusions and achieved in 2009/10 rates around half the national average.

The project's final seminar was set up as a confidential event for eight groups: the five project LAs which had a record of high exclusion rates; two of the low excluding LAs and the project team. Each had different perspective and experiences.

The project focus on exclusions at LA level was the result of three motivating factors: firstly, a conviction that education power and control is exercised to an important degree at the corporate level through elected members and officers; secondly, the top 15 LA excluders had an average permanent exclusion rate seven times higher than the average for the 15 lowest excluders; thirdly, low excluders appeared to be able to maintain their low excluder position over time. There is, therefore, an LA dynamic at work. It was reasoned that if an LA's ways of working with its schools can be strengthened and better targeted, there should be a multiplier effect in reducing school exclusions. This is partly borne out by the project's experience and the achievements of the LAs.

Permanent exclusions were reduced in the five LAs. It must be acknowledged that this is through *their* efforts rather than the project's. Fixed term exclusion increased nationally but three of the LAs were able to reduce their rates of fixed term exclusions and were coming down further by 2009/10. The forces pushing up exclusions make for an extensive list. It is these which must be countered to reduce the rates of both permanent and fixed term exclusion.

As an action research project, this counts as a success in achieving, with the LAs, reduced exclusions. It was important to follow up, so as to discover if gains made were held and if a momentum for inclusion was sustained. Importantly, it corroborated and evidenced the means by which exclusions can be reduced and the importance of working at the level of the LA and cluster groups of schools with their attendant agencies. With changes in LA finances and role indicated in early drafts of the coalition administration education legislation, new formations of schools and other education providers may need to be created to manage these processes.

6

Interim conclusions

Introduction

The key strategic role of the LA is recognised and confirmed in this research and development project. The LA, or some agreed 'hub', is central to the management of those children and young people for whom mainstream school is challenging. The LA or hub cajoles and co-ordinates, sets up and maintains collaborative provision across the statutory and voluntary sector, often acts as the change agent, or recognises the need for one, and is the location of the key front line driver for the reduction in exclusions. The LA retains a political, financial and even moral power amongst the various providers of services for children, including education. Either the LA or a more localised partnership management arrangement can establish and sustain community based inclusion.

As presented in Figures 5.1 and 5.2, there was success in the five formerly high excluding areas, a tribute to the LAs themselves, in reducing exclusions between the baseline year and the final year of the project's operations. More striking was the continued improvement in exclusion statistics in the two years following the project. Viewed graphically, the reductions in permanent exclusion look impressive, though short of the targets set. The results for fixed term exclusions are less impressive but continued to improve up to the latest figures in 2009/10. Figures 5.3 and 5.4 showed that already low excluding LAs could maintain that record and even give attention to reducing fixed period exclusions.

Concerns have been raised about whether schools should pay for exclusions. They already do! Whether 'top-sliced', fined or seeing the LA pay for PRUs, the finance is coming from the General School Budget. LAs have historically been the commissioners for services for SEN, exclusions and other services. This downward commissioning from the LA to schools may change as LA financial controls are slackened and as, or if, more schools leave LA control. The expectation is that there will be more upward commissioning from schools and partnerships of schools.

Partnership strategies for reducing exclusions

More important than the schematic representation of these reductions, the project's work made it possible to evidence the major forces at work and the key factors involved. Major conclusions reached in the project's work through data gathered and analysed and tested out in seminar discussions involving the five high excluding LAs and two of the low excluders include the following:

- The LA is a key strategic force in the direction of education locally. It has the power to set the tone and influence the culture. Elected members and officers have the capacity to engage robustly and constructively with their schools and develop cooperative and effective ways of working with the most challenging children and young people

- There are no specific off the shelf packages to be implemented to solve the high excluding problem, which will work in ignorance of historical and relationship factors within the LA

- Solutions have to be worked for and driven collaboratively by LA officers and schools. Changes have to come from the local area, supported strategically but managed with confidence by those on the ground and in the know

- Low excluding LAs see themselves as strategic partners within the education community (the wider grouping of education including schools, facilities, and statutory and voluntary agencies, of which school partnerships are a part) rather than as controlling organisations. This perception promotes co-operation and facilitates change

- Political backing is vital and can back reductions in exclusion informed by arguments which are simultaneously *moral, economic* and about *professional pride*: the moral concerns about not rejecting some young people and adversely affecting their life chances; the economic argument about exclusionary policies which are expensive (PRU places cost at about three times as much as a mainstream school place); professional pride is that schools, with their children's services partners, are capable of maintaining almost all behaviourally chal-

lenging pupils in mainstream education and sustaining their engagement with education – however creatively that is done

■ There is the need for robust, sustained pressure on, and negotiation
with, schools by LA officers who are senior and influential enough to
sit at the table with secondary school headteachers and able to re-
allocate some resources. One key, powerful, senior mediating officer,
who has director and cabinet backing has been vital in those LAs
achieving low rates of permanent exclusion. These localised strategic
functions can be played out with sub-LA level arrangements and are
increasingly found in the larger LAs

■ Certain financial drivers are used too little, in terms of schools' own
budgets, partnership or cluster budgets and LA pockets of funding.
Should a school with a surplus, particularly when above the DfE proposed limit of 5% (8% for primary schools), be permitted to exclude
a pupil permanently?

Forces which raise exclusions

It was evident that a range of forces operate to push up exclusions and some
can be fairly changeable over time, sometimes influenced by national political swings or the pronouncements of a minister

An implicit exclusionary culture

The judgement made that the child's behaviour requires an exclusion from
school and the unthinking application of the exclusion machinery underpins
permanent exclusion.

The standards agenda

The pressure on heads to raise and maintain standards can lead to a lack of
will to invest in pupils who display challenging behaviour. The fact that some
headteachers with their staff and with other professionals *have* accomplished
both indicates that there is not the inevitable choice between high attainment
and inclusion.

Staff training

The school workforce needs individually and collectively to broaden skills
and increase tolerance and understanding to cater for the full range of young
people, including the behaviourally challenging.

Behaviour that is very risky

The incidence of pupils carrying guns and knives and involved in gang culture poses particular difficulties and the safety of pupils has to be ensured. Drugs – possessing and supplying – constitute challenges at national and school level. The allowed response of exclusion is not usually the best option.

Getting the multiagency support

It was recognised as a recurring concern for those working with challenging youngsters that getting support from other agencies was still difficult and getting *joined up* action more difficult still. This differed from area to area and in some cases it was it was not that more multiagency help was available in low excluding areas but that they had ways of compensating for the lack and the gaps.

The myth of eliciting support for the child

Some headteachers will say, 'I excluded them so they will get the support they needs'. LA staff will argue that it is well known that this is not a solution. Indeed, in contexts where relationships are poorly developed between LA officers and schools, LA staff will resist responding quickly and positively lest they feed the myth!

Parental non-cooperation

When parents do not cooperate, heads are known to say, 'They've rejected all the help we have offered'. The exclusion is seen as a last resort. The view can be taken that not enough effort is made or other professionals skilled at working with parents are not co-opted or not available.

Day 6 agenda

There is evidence that Day 6 provision is a driver for additional permanent exclusions. Some LA officers thought it was, whilst a number of headteachers said it was not. However, it was pointed out that since the Day 6 provision rules would *not* be considered legitimate justification for a permanent exclusion, many heads would feel that saying this was a contributory factor was politically incorrect, and were reluctant to admit this to researchers. What is incontrovertible is that some primary phase heads did admit to researchers that Day 6 provision rules were something which hastened a permanent exclusion decision. Arguably, there should be Day 1 provision and some LAs in BIP areas aimed for this. The Day 6 (why 6?) provision has the look of a peculiar compromise, unlikely to last but saving some money, avoiding the need to think more deeply and potentially having perverse consequences.

The one-off incident

About a third of permanent exclusions from schools are of pupils who were not registered as at risk of permanent exclusion. The incident might involve extreme violence, drugs or bringing a weapon onto the school premises. It is possible to conceive of protocols whereby headteachers can ensure the safety of their staff and pupils without the need for the legalistic and punitive act of exclusion. In some local authorities, and in some schools, the use of exclusions for drug offences is used less than in others.

Allocation and use of deprivation funding

The distribution of deprivation funding between least and most deprived schools may not favour the latter enough. Funds in school budgets related to social deprivation are not necessarily being used to address deprivation issues and often are not targeted at the right young people. Acceptance is growing slowly that some pupils are more expensive to educate and look after than others. Spending relatively large amounts on meeting the needs of small groups of children is a necessary part of reducing exclusions.

Action Planning

Confirming work on this project and extending earlier work (Abdelnoor, 1999; Parsons, 1999), the generic solutions remain in eight areas:

1. generating a strategic, holistic, long term view – *the big picture*
2. shared commitment across schools and LA members and officers – *explicit principles and procedures*
3. making more diverse and multi-level provision in schools – *broaden the school*
4. managed moves and school cluster responsibilities – *build the bridges*
5. alternative provision – *find or make a place for every child*
6. multi-agency working – *joining up the dots*
7. ethos and attitudes – *sharing a vision*
8. commitment to collective organisation for at risk young people – *maintaining the hub*

What is crucial is how an LA and its schools, clusters of schools or children's trusts work this through – and front line LA officers doing business with their schools is central to working out satisfactory arrangements that will endure.

1. Generating a strategic, holistic, long term view – *the big picture*

Taffinder (1999) is convincing in his argument that local and individual action is fundamentally motivated by understanding where a strategy fits and the broad range of reasons for it. Headteachers, teachers and other agents need to see the social purpose of education, the moral purpose of social care and the unequal impact of actions like exclusion on particular groups in society. They need to see also the longer term damage and the costs to society of allowing the emergence of young people who are ill-equipped to work, relate or manage themselves.

2. Shared commitment across schools and LA members and officers – *explicit principles and procedures*

Fundamental to the school inclusion effort are LA councillor support and agreed principles and protocols with schools. Key principles include protocols and mechanisms for the allocation of hard to place pupils. A number of objective scoring schemes, sometimes with finance attached, are available and can be negotiated to work with groups of headteachers.

Schools require speedy advice and action from LA officers at times of crisis over a pupil's behaviour. Where this is provided, confidence increases and exclusions are minimised. There was a feeling that if schools in an area, comprising a partnership or cluster, were to accept shared ownership of *all* children in their area as an underlying principle this would enable transfers and movement of pupils to be arranged in a more caring and beneficial way.

Where a body of opinion can be established amongst headteachers about the proper way to proceed, fair sharing of difficult pupils and the procedures to be followed, colleagues can be brought into line by pressure from fellow headteachers. School Improvement Partners and other consultants available to the school were an important resource which was probably under-utilised. Economic cuts from 2011 will mean far fewer of these.

3. Making more diverse and multi-level provision in schools – *broaden the school*

Headteachers are the legal agents making decisions on school exclusions. It is important to determine how far alterations in values and practices at school level might alter exclusion habits. While it is acknowledged that there is a 'hearts and minds' job to be done with schools by the local authority, there is also the need to encourage schools to set up their own layers of provision (inclusion units etc), entertain managed moves and engage in more creative thinking about alternative curricula. One contributor noted that 'it can be disaffection from a poor curriculum that causes the problem' and that improved curriculum has to go hand in hand with work with pupils and parents.

Flexibility of provision needs to be created and supported by schools and the Local Authority. This includes the use of social deprivation money in schools to set up units, employ learning mentors, fund alternative provision etc, and the movement into and out of alternative provision and Pupil Referral Units needs to be kept fluid.

There is a caring, developmental and supportive role for schools and LA personnel, particularly with children whose preparation for school or family support circumstances for school are limited and often at the root of their difficulties with surviving in school. While nurture groups are more often found in infant schools to prepare reception children, some secondary schools have actually developed classes which serve this function at their level.

Finance received by schools, portions of which are allocated for social deprivation, may not be appropriately used. One can raise questions about the extent to which schools spend their social deprivation money on the relevant children. In earlier pages, examples of schools are described where a complex array of additional facilities are provided and a more varied workforce employed to better meet the needs of challenging young people.

There is an ongoing need to give teachers confidence in themselves to develop relational skills to work with young people with challenging behaviour. In initial teacher education and continuing professional development, too great an emphasis is placed on *behaviour* policies and *discipline* policies, both of which place the problem with the young person. *Relationship* policies would suggest a shared responsibility!

It is also necessary to overcome the divide that is currently manifest in the minds of education managers between the deserving, assessed special educational needs pupil and the undeserving EBD pupil. Overriding this involves the school and its associated services taking the responsibility to meet the full range of needs evident in its school community.

4. Managed moves and school cluster responsibilities – *build the bridges*

Adam Abdelnoor's book, published through The Gulbenkian Foundation, is available online (see references). A managed move is more than the simple transfer of a pupil from one school to another. It can be seen as an organised consensual movement of the pupil from school to school but maybe from school to alternative provision, or to the PRU or some other monitored and regulated provision. An important element in it is the emphasis on meeting need and a great diminution in the exercise of punishment.

It was emphasised that there should be a risk assessment before a managed move. It was evident that the full implementation of community based inclusion had some way to go in the practice. In most LAs, practices, in which parent consultation, review, establishing induction and support arrangements in the receiving school and management of any breakdown are not in place as routine.

It is not yet clear that subgroups of schools in LAs are generally ready to operationalise a managed transfer system unaided. The history of cooperative working, especially over 'difficult pupils' is not firmly in place. There is every prospect that this can be developed and new arrangements following the Education White paper, 2010 encourage this.

5. Alternative provision – *find or make a place for every child*

There was considerable debate about what would count as satisfactory alternative provision, how it would be monitored and quality assured, and how attendance would be ensured. Some low excluding LAs have developed a range of alternative provision for children who are out of school and for children who can no longer be managed in school and who would ordinarily be excluded but are allocated to these facilities. A DVD (North Lincolnshire 2007) can be viewed on Teachers TV. It shows a farm experience which pupils receive for one day per week along with other tailored curriculum provision in school for the other four days. Reports from teachers, pupils and parents about alternative curriculum providers all gave evidence about the value of the right mix of personalised curricula, of which the alternative provision could be part. Consideration might be given to the 'waking hours curriculum', and *not-school.net* (described as an online Summerhill). Some schools have a TIF (temporary inclusive facility) which is schooling from 3-6 pm.

There are challenges in funding, costing, quality assuring and ensuring attendance at the alternative provision. Low excluding LA B has a stated expectation of high attendance (they achieve 80% attendance) and a certificated outcome. If the alternative provider does not satisfy these requirements, LA would stop using them. There were also differences among the attendees about what counted as *full-time provision.* Some believed 18 hours a week would be officially acceptable and others reported that a Joint Area Review required 23-25 hours a week.

At present, alternatives which can be provided for Key Stage 3 pupils are more limited than those available at Key Stage 4; where these are extended it helps to reduce exclusions. There needs to be a creative approach to alternative provision and a reconsideration of what counts as educational and developmental experiences, especially for children who find being in and behaving in school quite difficult. There are grounds for stretching the bounds of what would count as appropriate provision that keeps the child in touch with education and in a position to progress.

As Thomson and Russell (2007) show in their mapping of alternative provision, there is work to be done in regularising this loose array of provision. There are signs that where it is taken seriously it can work with parent consultation, accreditation routes, monitoring and some transition to different forms of provision. At best, it is managed through schools with the other parts provided in-house, even if separately organised, in order to ensure a balance and basic skills acquisition.

6. Multi-agency working – *joining up the dots*
Multi-agency working means engaging with the full range of children's services including the voluntary sector. With Every Child Matters, Children's Services Directorates and Local Children's Services Partnerships the expectations of and opportunities for joined-up working are great. The ability to call on or arrange speedy referral to other professionals is developing. Some schools are discarding the notion of referral as it passes the problem on, but regard working with other professionals as a collaboration for the benefit of the child where the school retains the responsibility. The extended school, the full service school and the community school all carry the overlapping expectation that the school stretches its remit and that teachers see themselves as part of a multi-agency team.

Schools need access to high quality intervention and prevention work. While there is a problem with outsiders coming in to solve problems with young people, there have been many instances of well respected external consultants working with groups, with teachers and with individuals, modelling the ways to work best with pupils. Other schemes involving staff training or the application of particular methods with groups have reaped benefits. It was said that in respect of external support, 'money talks and size matters'; the allocation of funding and the size of teams offering support make a difference to schools' responses to challenging behaviour from children in their schools.

Multi-agency working needs to be a reality and not an aspiration. Too often the principles of multi-agency working are set and agreements made at a strategic level, but the aspiration is insufficiently driven through to practical implementation. The creation of small teams working in a case work manner (see low excluding LA C) are proving effective. Locality based teams with defined case loads regularly monitored and assessed are proving effective; at best, these are integrated into the working of schools. Specifically, it can be said:

- In principle, multi-professional teams are seen as effective, whereas 'multiagency strategies' are unlikely to be implemented *in the absence of multi-professional teams*
- A multi-professional team is made up of a group of practitioners from different agencies that share a work-base, and collaboratively agree shared agendas and action plans
- This locality base and focus, which might be the newly developing Children's Centre or based in a school, holds promise but will need to be robustly worked through and monitored
- *Every Child Matters*, the creation of Children and Families Directorates and the strategic plans which go with them, often slow progress on specific targets. It is important not to expect structural changes to bring about the reductions in exclusions without specific measures and public will in place.

The implementation of Children's Trusts should provide a locality based focus and hub for much of the supportive work needed to help youngsters who present behavioural challenges. During this project, some of the pupils and parents interviewed revealed considerable insights into their own situations. They are partners in the process and not simply the problem. Conflict resolution is needed in a number of areas to reconcile parties to working productively together; this can include overcoming difficulties between education and children's social care as well as between teachers and parents.

7. Ethos and attitudes – *sharing a vision*

This could have been the starting position, working at hearts and minds to gain support for including all children and responding to all needs. It may be an initial stimulus to set in place explicit principles and procedures but the pragmatics operating strongly suggest that, if you can make it work first, then practical support and buy-in will follow and the appropriate values will emerge to reinforce developing successful practice. Headteachers will all say they do not want to exclude and arguably the preferred moral position is sub-scribed to but not activated. Showing it can work allows the moral power to connect with the practical and strategic drive to continue the education of all those who make up their school population.

8. Commitment to collective organisation for at risk young people – *maintaining the hub*

Whether it is the LA or another formalised arrangement, for community based inclusion to work the organisational facility that designs, maintains and manages the collective system has to cater for the educational needs of *all* pupils in the area. This may have at its core the Fair Access Committee, meeting very regularly and dispensing business quickly. It should be attended by mediating professionals who may need to ease transitions or assess further the suitability or readiness of a pupil for a particular setting. It may involve voting! It may have control of resources. It should certainly be the forum for ascertaining what services should be commissioned and monitor transparently what is happening, who moves where and from where. There is evidence that this collaboration amongst a local set of education providers works, whether across a small unitory LA or at the level of sub-LA groupings.

Figure 6.1 illustrates an inclusive arrangement where the boundary is around a group of schools and other agents operating in the field of child care and education. This is also the boundary for finance and the central hub is the vital operational heart of the system.

Messages to stakeholders

The main groups which need to respond are the school clusters with asso-ciated Children's Trusts, local authorities and the Department for Education. The articulation of complementary policies and practice across these three levels should ensure that the education and care of behaviourally challenging children is better managed.

Messages for parents, carers, children and young people

You deserve to be heard, to have your needs considered, to be treated fairly and to have the best interests of the young people at the centre of discussions driving decisions. The state education system should be designed to address the needs and challenges presented by every learner, and professional people are trained and paid to do so as public servants. Most young people who are challenging at school are challenging at home and the best way forward is an alliance between home and school which seeks to a achieve this, and in ways

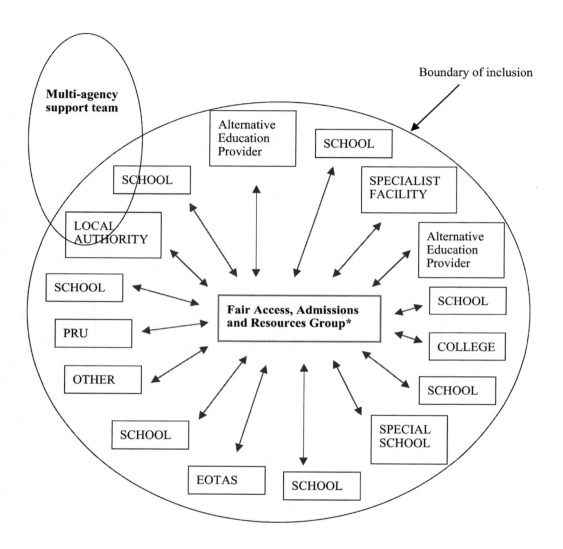

Figure 6.1: Schools, education providers and support professionals operating through a hub

that do not entail legal representation and appeals – though sadly it sometimes comes to that.

Messages for school clusters

Within schools, more attention needs to be given to support for behaviourally challenging young people, with better developed in-school arrangements for therapeutic work, isolation and restoration. This needs to be matched by routine ways of managing transfers in a conciliatory and participative way and for the use of alternative provision. Schools will need to adjust funding and allocate resources disproportionately to this small number of young people. Most will have funds for this, allocated in various ways by the LA according to a formula which acknowledges the social deprivation of the school's intake.

Schools will need to *really* establish cooperative protocols in which *all* (secondary) schools participate. Collectively, they will need to build an acceptance that all the children belong to this community and that if they do have to move, the schools work to ensure this is supported and that if the prospect of a return is kept open, the school maintains contact. School cluster or local delivery partnership arrangements are not firmly established and, if managed within themselves (ie not having a coordinating agent), it seems unlikely that progress in preventing school exclusions would be quick and assured.

Messages for local authorities

There is a need for staff who can do business with heads to be present in schools and available to the people who can support schools in extending their provision and efforts for inclusion and who have a sufficiently powerful voice back at County/Town Hall to elicit more resources when necessary. Elsewhere, it has been suggested that there is a need for an 'interagency czar' operating in what is called a 'Stalinist environment' (Parsons and Hailes, 2004), with political backing and focused street level work regularly monitored.

Messages for the Department for Education

There is confusion about policy and the complexity of policy which has to be addressed at the local level. League tables are a hindrance and there should be less emphasis on standards. There needs to be encouragement and allowance for more alternatives for Key Stage 3. Day 6 provision is problematic and unhelpful. The punitive tendency in some policies (see Parsons, 2005) runs counter to a position which is about meeting unmet needs, restorative approaches and preventative arrangements in schools and LAs.

The moral and financial imperatives

Permanent exclusion is a punishment and it damages pupils. It is a formal rejection of the child. It is not designed to address the child's needs. It is a casting off of the responsibility of mainstream schools collectively to manage the continued education of all their pupils. Fixed term exclusions, except for medical (including cooling off) reasons, are also damaging, often putting children further behind in school work, learning and social acceptance. If further evidence were needed on damage to children then one need go no further than Arnold *et al* (2009) for graphic accounts of the experience of exclusion for children and families.

A permanent exclusion is a process which has no forward plan. There is frequently a hiatus and loss of education and direction for the child. A transfer, respite or a managed move that is acceptably carried out always includes a forward plan and is, therefore, distinctly different from an exclusion.

If the Every Child Matters and Children's Rights perspective is not sufficiently powerful to convince schools and LAs, then the financial perspective might be. Firstly, there is the bald fact that a PRU place and other substitute education costs around three times the amount for a school place, and PRU attainment outcomes generally are not high. Secondly, the marginalisation of these young people often brings with it at the same time other calculable expense as other services are called upon. Thirdly, there is the matter of longer term costs about which for the most part we can only speculate. But they include crime, mental health, unemployment and unemployability, struggling relationships and inadequate parenting. Education and child social care services can do much to reduce the likelihood of adverse consequences, be it for moral or for financial motives.

7

An inclusion agenda for
the local authority

Introduction

This final section sets out an agenda for strategic action for a local authority which seeks to reduce its permanent and fixed term exclusions. It is illustrated with examples drawn from the low excluding local authorities and erstwhile high excluders who are moving to better solutions. It covers the layers and connected strategic elements which need attention if this goal is to be achieved and low or nil permanent exclusions are to be maintained.

The action, which it may be necessary to build over a two year period, has a number of overlapping and interlocking elements. Whilst it may have one or two moderately senior officers who are the drivers, there need to be alliances which will support and sustain the growing pressure and capacity to make appropriate provision for all children in the local authority. It is suggested that thinking about strategic action can be grouped under the headings below, extending the discussion from chapter 6.

1. *the big picture*
2. *explicit principles and procedures*
3. *broaden the school*
4. *build the bridges*
5. *find or make a place for every child*
6. *join up the dots*
7. *share a vision*
8. *maintain the hub*

Currently, it could be said that nationally and locally, in official decision-making locations as well as in pubs and clubs, there is pressure towards punitive responses, as represented in Figure 7.1 below. A punitive stance is likely to lead to reluctance to spend, or to think creatively about provision for young people with challenging behaviour. This in turn leads to neglect and a diminution of life chances and on to increasing the likelihood that more such young people will come through the poorly functioning systems.

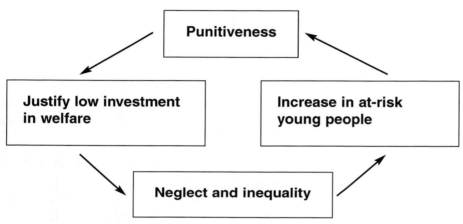

Figure 7.1: the vicious school exclusion cycle
(adapted from Parsons, 2005)

The sections below illustrate the strategic action at LA level and propose eight strategic components likely to enhance the chances of low exclusions, a retreat from punitive stances, morally questionable state parenting and waste of public money.

1. The big picture

The overarching purpose of inclusive schooling needs to be articulated locally. The community-wide consequences of poorly educated and rejected young people needs to be grasped. The capacity for partnerships of schools, other education providers and social care professionals to manage community based inclusion needs to be established.

2. Explicit principles and procedures

The political voice is vitally important. Committing the LA to being a low or nil excluding area has to be established at the level of elected members.

Our contact across the eight local authorities, and with others, indicated the importance of local authority councillors, particularly the cabinet member for education, being actively supportive of reducing exclusions and finding alternative ways of managing the continued education of some challenging and troubled children. Examples are given from low excluding LAs B and C and from LA 2. An instance of how this can play out in another local authority is illustrated in the cameo below.

Cameo 7.1: Political Backing for Reductions in Exclusions

The inclusion officer for the authority had visited the school to criticise a permanent exclusion decision and press for its overturn. The headteacher contacted his local councillor to complain and asked the councillor to raise this in the chamber. The councillor duly reported critically on the inclusion officer at the full council meeting, where he was told 'this is an inclusive local authority'. He was instructed to go back to his headteacher and tell the headteacher to find other ways of managing problems of this sort and desist from permanent exclusion unless problems with a pupil were very much more serious.

Strategic component 1: Identify the credible inclusion champion at LA member level.

Strategic decisions made by the LA can have far reaching consequences for the relationship with schools and the care and education for children and young people who are excluded or are at risk of exclusion. The reminder by a public representative that headteachers are public servants paid to provide education for the local population of young people can have its place; it is not all amicable shared decision-making and there is a place for reminders about what people's jobs are.

Cameo 7.2: Schools are public institutions in place to serve the local area

In LA4, the cabinet member for education was acutely aware of the competing pressures for reducing exclusions and for maintaining standards of attainment At a LA headteacher conference, she described how she was going to tell heads that, as leaders of their schools on £80,000, £90,000 or £100,000, they should be taking responsibility for the education of the children who come to them and not picking and choosing whom they would wish to educate.

The wholesale change of provision can send strong signals. This is not something to impose but it needs forceful leadership and confidence to bring it about.

Cameo 7.3: PRUs for pupils not excluded from school

The decision was taken in one local authority 'over a weekend' to change the admission rules for the pupil referral unit. Previously, a pupil could only go to the PRU if they had been permanently excluded. The decision was to change the rule so a pupil could only go to the PRU if they had *not* been permanently excluded. This led to an expected rise in young people who were referred to and were taken in by the PRU but this number quickly dropped and provision is now in place for managed transfers to the PRU and back in to schools and other arrangements in a more orderly and less crisis driven fashion than had been the case before. This local authority had been a slightly above average excluder; now it permanently excludes at one quarter the national rate of permanent exclusions.

Strategic component 2: Speedily negotiate authority level changes in structures, provision and staffing that headteachers will accept.

Strategic component 3: Ensure the lead is taken by a high ranking and well-paid officer who has the authority and respect of heads and who can confront them when contrary decisions are made but can also deliver some funding and director and cabinet level backing and validation.

3. Broaden the school

Strategic component 4: Support school leaders in diversifying their provision and making best use of the diversified workforce in supporting challenging young people and their families.

4. Build the bridges

This is about making the transfer to another place of learning a secure, planned and restorative experience. Abdelnoor (2007) refers to this as 'community based inclusion', where the education centres, schools, PRUS and alternative provision work together, with shared values and a common purpose.

Strategic component 5: establish agreement amongst schools about how pupils might be moved from their current school, either permanently or temporarily, building on personal relations between schools but creating fair access protocols or points systems.

There is the argument that exclusions can be greatly cut artificially by telephoning headteachers before an exclusion takes effect, and asking for the child to be referred to the PRU or Alternative Curriculum without needing to go through the permanent exclusion process. Some see this as fiddling the figures and simply getting a permanent exclusion by another name. This need not be, and increasingly is not, the case. Managed properly and transparently, managed moves should epitomise the best in the care of every child. PRUs still have a part to play but it is a calmly managed transfer that is the way forward and this requires carefully worked out protocols.

5. Find or make a place for every child
Alternative curriculum and personalised learning are an integral part of the education community's provision. The LA is well placed to determine the providers available and the range of provision needs to be mediated, brokered and quality assured.

Strategic component 6: develop a range of alternative curriculum providers, assessing and monitoring that gaps in need are filled and that the providers can meet targets and contribute valuably to children's development including qualifications.

6. Joining up the dots
A range of agencies have a part to play in the support of children, schools and families where a child's retention in the school is becoming challenging. Schools have often had the idea that 'someone out there can fix this child', but this has been unhelpful all round. The pupil needs help to function better in the school context and within sets of existing relationships. BESTs, BIPS, MASTs etc can support and ease transfers and reintegration where this is necessary.

Strategic component 7: Ensure that the teams of other professionals are of appropriate skill levels and can offer a fast response where problems occur.

7. Sharing a vision
The shared vision is a return to the explicit principles and procedures but is also a confirmation of the commitment to provide for all. And it is a call to publicly reaffirm and to celebrate local achievements in terms of the demonstrated ability to ensure that 'every child matters'

Strategic component 8: Create and recreate the sense of belief in the LA's duty to provide calmly and restoratively for every child no matter what the challenges.

8. Maintain the hub

Either the LA or a local arrangement covering a small number of secondary schools and their primary feeder schools needs to be established to enable collaboration across schools. Diminishing LA finance and influence and the 'localism' promoted urge the move towards consortia of headteachers operating as agents for the community and not just for their individual schools. Tightly managed cross-school arrangements are necessary, and optimism is fuelled by experience of local consortia and the fact that academies are acting as full partners in some of these.

Concluding note

Exclusions, whether for a fixed period or permanently, are not a necessary part of the school's discipline policy when managed within an education community and with a strong, consultative, supportive lead from LA officers and politicians. It is prudent to accept a third way 'affordability and solidarity' solution which involves the compromise of wanting all to be in mainstream and accepting that the costs need to be limited, if political support is to be maintained and insecure middle classes are to remain supportive. This means striking a balance between support for challenging young people while also accepting that there are financial limits.

While watchful of this balance, it is reasonable to ague that there is greater investment yet to be made on supporting our vulnerable and challenging young people; deprivation money is often not being spent on addressing deprivation issues, school budgets are often underspent and LAs overspend on expensive, inevitably underachieving, PRUs. Moreover, acceptance is growing that costs to the full range of public services on expensive, inevitably underachieving PRUs, even in the medium term, would be lowered by more preventative work and less punitive responses. The policies on the small number of children excluded or at risk of exclusion from school are ever in flux and we need to be mindful not just of the possibilities of numbers of exclusion increasing but also of the righteousness that has often accompanied the whole business of exclusion. This has been couched in terms of the deservingness and necessity of the ejection and rejection and the worthlessness of the child and the family.

Applying *Every Child Matters* and the UN Convention on the Rights of the Child would have greater force and lead to a climate of opinion where far fewer children were imprisoned and pupil exclusion from school would not happen.

Recognising the political third way, there are no absolutes. Instead, there is incremental change, wearing down punitive attitudes and changing harmful policies. Figure 7.2 is a diagram of the virtuous circle which might operate at local and national level. Progress through these interventions could develop a cycle which begins with prevention, support and restorative commitments, leads on to greater investment in young people's welfare, building to an environment of caring and equity and resulting in reduced numbers of 'at risk' young people.

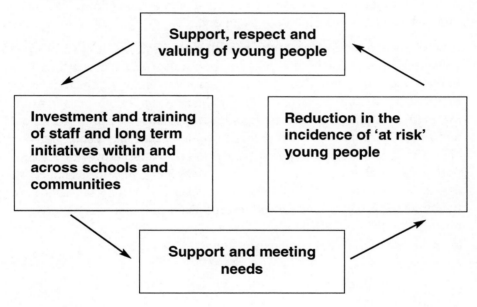

Figure 7.2: the virtuous child support and inclusion cycle

This book is about rendering exclusions unnecessary through the provision of varied provision in schools, alternative provision and managed moves with multiagency working to support children and families in difficulties. The Steer reports (2005; 2009) are, as one might expect, focused on schools and school staff and pupils. The 2009 report makes reference to legal powers (to remain unaltered), parents, children's trusts and partnerships. It is in these last areas in the move to community full service extended schools, addressing child poverty and social justice issues of lower attainment and exclusions experienced by deprived neighbourhoods that much greater development and commitment is sought. Joined up policy needs to acknowledge, at the one end of the spectrum, that troubled young people need a key adult addressing attachment disorders (Bomber, 2007) and at the other, the real challenges of broad social inclusion at the level of communities (DWP, 2006).

It is evident that, whatever arrangements a local authority makes to provide for the continuing education of its pupils, there has to be a sign-up from the schools. This has to be matched by local authority staffing capacity to support schools in their work with young people and access to a range of other professionals to help meet the challenges that behaviourally troubled young people present. Short term projects and the reliance on external organisations would not seem to offer much by way of long term help to bring down exclusions and make better provision for these children.

A lot of good work goes on at the vital strategic level, but it must proceed powerfully beyond that level; it must co-opt headteachers at the earliest stage to make ready the ground for co-operative implementation. Much depends on the right mix of messages from local politicians, senior officers and front-line staff. It also requires the management of resources close to the school and child. The alternatives to exclusion maintain a relationship with the child, are collaborative with parents and other education providers, are supportive of the child's general and social development, maximise chances of educational success and diminish the prospects of anti-social behaviour, unemployment and troubled relationships. Even minimal interpretation of the Rights of the Child demands that we apply our intelligence and resources to ensure social and educational inclusion.

References

Abdelnoor, A (1999) *Preventing Exclusions*. Oxford: Heinemann

Abdelnoor, A (2007) *Managed Moves: A complete guide to managed moves as an alternative to permanent exclusion.* London: Calouste Gulbenkian Foundation www.gulbenkian.org.uk/media/ item/1229/ 110/Managed-moves.pdf (accessed 21.010.08)

Arnold, C., Yeomans, J. and Simpson, S. with Solomon, M. (2009) *Excluded from School: complex discourses and psychological perspectives,* Stoke on Trent: Trentham Books

Balls, E (2008) Ed Balls announces early support to keep pupils on track. DCSF news release 23 October 2008, 2008/0237. http://www.dcsf.gov.uk/pns/DisplayPN.cgi?pn_id=2008_0237 (accessed 01.02.09)

Bomber, L M (2007) *Inside I'm Hurting: practical strategies for supporting children with attachment difficulties in school.* London: Worth Publishing

DCSF (2007a) *Improving Behaviour and Attendance: Guidance on Exclusion from Schools and Pupil Referral Units.* London: Department for Children, Schools and Families. www.teachernet. gov.uk/wholeschool/behaviour/exclusion/guidance2007/ (accessed 07.07.08)

DCSF (2007b) T*he Children's Plan: Building Brighter Futures.* London: Department for Children, Schools and Families. www.dcsf.gov.uk/publications/childrensplan/downloads/The_Childrens_ Plan.pdf (accessed 07.07.08)

DCSF (2007c) *Design principle 2: schools agree fair access and managed moves protocols and works with local authorities to provide school places.* London: Department for Children, Schools and Families. www.teachernet.gov.uk/wholeschool/behaviour/collaboration/guidance/designprinciples/further information/

DCSF (2008a) *Back on Track: A strategy for modernising alternative provision for young people.* London: Department for Children, Schools and Families. www.dcsf.gov.uk/publications/ backontrack/pdfs/7668-DCSF-BackonTrackWEB.pdf (accessed 22.02.09)

DCSF (2008b) *Improving Behaviour and Attendance: Guidance on Exclusion from Schools and Pupil Referral Units.* London: Department for Children, Schools and Families. www.behaviour4learning.ac.uk/ attachments/8a4d7e51-a132-496c-8e0d-70e2e49a72dd.pdf (accessed 01.02.09)

DCSF (2008c) *Behaviour4Learning.* www.behaviour4learning.ac.uk/viewarticle2.aspx?contentId= 10536 (accessed 13.04.09)

DCSF (2008d) *National Strategy – Behaviour and Attendance.* www.ttrb.ac.uk/viewarticle2.aspx?content Id=11202 (accessed 13.04.09)

DfE (2010) *The Importance of Teaching (Education White Paper),* London: Department for Education

DfEE (1999) *Social Inclusion: Pupil Support (SIPS) – Circular 10/99.* London: Department for Education and Employment

DfES (2004a) *Children Act 2004.* London: Department for Education and Skills. www.opsi.gov.uk/Acts/ acts2004/ukpga_20040031_en_12 (accessed 21.06.07)

DfES, (2004a) *Behaviour and Attendance.* London: Department for Education and Skills

DfES, (2004b) *Improving Behaviour and Attendance: Guidance on Exclusion from Schools and Pupil Referral Units.* London: Department for Education and Skills

DfES, (2004c) *Guidance on Exclusion from Schools and Pupil Referral Units.* London: Department for Education and Skills

DfES (2005) *Higher Standards, Better Schools for All* (Education White Paper). London: Department for Education and Skills

DWP (2006) *Working Together: UK National Action Plan on Social Inclusion 2006-08.* London: Department for Work and Pensions. www.dwp.gov.uk/publications/dwp/2006/nap/Working Together.pdf (accessed 08.12.07)

Ellis, S and Tod, J (2009) *Behaviour for Learning.* London: David Fulton

Hallam, S and Rogers, L (2008) *Improving Behaviour and Attendance at School.* Maidenhead: Open University Press

Hook, P and Vass, A (2000) *Confident classroom leadership.* London: David Fulton

North Lincolnshire Local Authority (2007) *Secondary Special Needs – Working to Learn* (DVD). www. teachers.tv/video/3369 (accessed 11.11.08)

Ofsted (2009) *Day six of exclusion: the extent and quality of provision for pupils.* London: Ofsted. www.ofsted.gov.uk/Ofsted-home/Publications-and-research/Browse-all-by/Documents-by-type/Thematic-reports/Day-six-of-exclusion-the-extent-and-quality-of-provision-for-pupils (accessed 15.05.09)

Parsons, C (1999) *Education, Exclusion and Citizenship.* London: Routledge

Parsons, C (2005) School Exclusions: the will to punish. *British Journal of Educational Studies* 53(2) p187-211

Parsons, C (2009) Explaining sustained inequalities in ethnic minority school exclusion in England. *Oxford Review of Education* 35(2) p249-265

Parsons, C. (2010) Achieving zero permanent exclusions from school, social justice and economy, *FORUM,* 52.3 p395-404

Parsons, C, Annan, G, Cornwall, J, Godfrey, R, Hepburn, S and Wennerstrom, V (2005) *Minority Ethnic Exclusions and the Race Relations (Amendment) Act, 2000,* Research Report 616. London: Department for Education and Skills. www.dfes.gov.uk/research/data /uploadfiles/RR616.pdf (accessed 24.06.07)

Parsons, C and Hailes, J (2004) Voluntary Organisations and the Contribution to Social Justice in Schools: Learning from a Case Study. *Journal of Education Policy,* 19(4) p473-496

Parsons, C, Walraven, G, Day, C and van Veen, D (2000) *Combating Social Exclusion through Education: Authoritarianism, Laissez-faire or Third Way,* Leuven: Garant

Rogers, B (2006) *Classroom Behaviour.* London: Sage

Steer, A (2005) *Learning Behaviour.* London: Department for Education and Skills. www.dcsf.gov.uk/ behaviourandattendance/uploads/Learning%20Behaviour%20(published).pdf (accessed 10.10.08)

Steer, A (2009) *Learning Behaviour: the Report on the Practitioners' Group on School Behaviour and Discipline.* London: Department for Children, Schools and Families. http://publications.dcsf.gov.uk/ eOrderingDownload/Learning-Behaviour.pdf (accessed 16.04.09)

Taffinder, P. (1999) Big Change: a route-map for corporate transformation, Chichester: Wiley

Teachernet (2005) *Improving behaviour and tackling persistent truancy through schools working in collaboration.* www.teachernet.gov.uk/wholeschool/ behaviour/collaboration/ (accessed 01.02.09)

Teachernet (2008) *Get into Higher Education: Teaching materials for Years 9-11.* London: DCSF. www. teachernet.gov.uk/aimhigher (accessed 01.06.09)

Thomson, P and Russell, L (2007) *Mapping the alternatives to permanent exclusion.* York: Joseph Rowntree Foundation. www.jrf.org.uk/bookshop/details.asp?pubid=919 (accessed 11.09.08)

UNICEF (2007) *An overview of child well-being in rich countries* (Report Card 7). Florence: UNICEF Innocenti Research Centre. www.unicef-irc.org/publications/pdf/rc7_eng.pdf (accessed 20.05.09)

Watt, M (2009) Behaviour and exclusions in Scotland. *Children and Young People Now,* 26.01.09

Subject Index